We shall not cease from exploration

And the end of all our exploring

Will be to arrive where we started

And know the place for the first time.

Through the unknown, remembered gate. . . .

T. S. Eliot, "Little Gidding"

Taking Jesus at His Word

WHAT JESUS REALLY SAID
IN THE SERMON ON THE MOUNT

Addison Hodges Hart

WILLIAM B. EERDMANS PUBLISHING COMPANY

GRAND RAPIDS, MICHIGAN / CAMBRIDGE, U.K.

Published 2012 by

Wm. B. Eerdmans Publishing Co.

2140 Oak Industrial Drive N.E., Grand Rapids, Michigan 49505 /

P.O. Box 163, Cambridge CB3 9PU U.K.

Printed in the United States of America

17 16 15 14 13 12   7 6 5 4 3 2 1

Library of Congress Cataloging-in-Publication Data

Hart, Addison Hodges, 1956-

Taking Jesus at his word: what Jesus really said in the Sermon on the mount /
Addison Hodges Hart.

p.   cm.

ISBN 978-0-8028-6691-2 (pbk.: alk. paper)

1. Sermon on the mount — Criticism, interpretation, etc.   I. Title.

BT380.3.H37   2012

226.9′06 — dc23

2012005587

www.eerdmans.com

For

Solrunn

Contents

CONTENTS

Acknowledgments

———

Every book of this sort owes much to those who have inspired or educated the author. I have spent years meditating on the Sermon on the Mount, and numerous have been the companions who have meditated on it with me. I think of my professors and teachers, some of whom have died (for example, Henri Nouwen, one of my teachers at Harvard Divinity School nearly three decades ago), and some who are still living and teaching new generations of Christian pastors and teachers in the New Testament (especially those who teach at Trinity Episcopal School for Ministry in Ambridge, Pennsylvania). I trust that nothing in this book will discredit them, since any errors or oddities of interpretation are solely my own. I think also of the many students and congregants it has been my privilege over the years to teach, in six churches and four states. Their questions and insights have some place in this and other books I've written, and I've probably learned more from them through their shared experiences than they ever did from me through my lectures.

Lastly, I wish to thank the fine folks at William B. Eerdmans Publishing Company, one of the truly fine American religious publishers. It is a genuine privilege to have an association with them. Especially I wish to thank my editor, Mary Hietbrink, who has edited not only this text, but also both my earlier books. I don't believe she's ever made a suggestion I didn't adopt and which, I'm sure, only improved the final version. This is my thanks for her work on all three of my books.

1

Coming Back to the Sermon on the Mount

—∞∞—

There is a phrase that comes from T. S. Eliot's "Little Gidding," the concluding portion of his *Four Quartets*, which could well describe how the Sermon on the Mount strikes many of us. It is the phrase "the unknown, remembered gate." The Sermon on the Mount serves, in some ways, as a "gate" or doorway into the message of Jesus. It is full of passages that are remembered by many who have never stepped inside a church. "Blessed are the poor in spirit." "Blessed are the meek." "A city set on a hill cannot be hid." "Our Father who art in heaven. . . ." "You cannot serve God and mammon." "Judge not, that you be not judged." One could go on and on with such remembered, partially remembered, digested or only half-digested lines. The point is, the Sermon on the Mount is an address containing numerous memorable sentences and ideas. And yet, for all its being memorable, it is somehow unknown to us. Unknown, that is, in the sense of it being an address with far more to it than a set of welcome or unwelcome, quite often ignored platitudes. It is, in actuality and intent, a whole way of life that we are meant to ponder, absorb, and by means of which be transformed.

It is to this "unknown, remembered gate" that I wish to go now, and, if you are willing, I would like to bring you along with me.

If one desires to listen to Jesus, there is no better place to begin than with his words in the Sermon on the Mount. It is, as many have said, the clearest statement of his teachings. It stands in Matthew's Gospel as his "inaugural address"; and because that Gospel was wisely placed as the very first book in the New Testament, the Sermon on the Mount is our first introduction to all the teachings of Jesus.

Taking up three chapters of Matthew, it is the heart of his message of the kingdom of God (or the "kingdom of heaven," as Matthew more often renders it). It is called the "Sermon [singular] on the Mount," but it may actually be a compilation of many "sermons" of Jesus, patched together from numerous conferences and skillfully sewn together into one continuous monologue. It may well be that he said the same words many times in different contexts, repeating them often so that they might sink in, not be forgotten, and work on his disciples' minds. Luke 6, for example, gives us a "sermon on the plain," much of it paralleling Matthew's mountain talk. It seems natural enough to assume that a variety of locations served as good places for Jesus to retreat and teach his hearers.

My wish in the pages that follow is to go up to the mountain of Jesus' "sermon" in my imagination, notebook in hand, and put myself before Jesus' presence there. I have been there many times before, at all the stages in my life; and now, in midlife, I want to listen anew to him. I won't be hearing him as I did, say, at the age of seventeen or the age of thirty-five. I will hear him now as someone who has lived more than half my life, a life already full with experiences, sorrows, and joys.

In this book I don't wish to theologize too heavily or even attempt more biblical exegesis than is absolutely necessary for my aim. This is a book of reflections; and I want to put any tendency to rationalize and categorize to one side, as best I can, and try to hear Jesus speak. I do not wish to be as concerned with doctrines *about* Jesus in these pages as about the words *of* Jesus and their immediate impact on me, a man in his fifties who has lived a while. My aim is to take in his words with as few preconceptions as possible, although one is never entirely devoid of preconceptions. But, I would like just to listen, think, ruminate, and take notes. Then, in turn, offer my notations to you.

No one lives in a vacuum. Everyone has a personal history, and anyone of my age who comes before a great teacher brings along a veritable suitcase filled with failures, sadnesses, regrets, joys, hopes, loves of various sorts, both formal and informal education, political views, religious views, and so on. The point of coming to a great teacher is, in fact, to make sense of all these personal things as well as the world around one, and to learn to see everything and oneself in a new light. Perhaps, in that light, we see that some of our ideas need to fall by the wayside, that others might require adjustment, and that some convictions may even have been strengthened. But, in the final analysis (and every engagement with a great teacher *is* always an analysis), we look for fresh guidance.

For me, a Christian, the road invariably leads back to Jesus. I listen to the recorded words of other great seminal teachers and learn from them — the humor and tang of Chuang Tzu, the razor-like wisdom of Buddha, the probing dialogues of Socrates, and so on, right down the flowing succession of ages and cultures. All find their place in my admiration, and have my careful attention. But Jesus takes the center, and all others surround him. I am his disciple, though I acknowledge I am a flawed one. My one consolation is that most of his disciples are flawed in some way, anyway. At least I have company among peers.

So, I propose to go back up the mountain, with my troubles and woes and all, and take notes. I want Jesus' words to level me, weigh me, draw me out of my rut, and force me to ask questions — both of him and of myself. I want the enlightenment he gives. I want to be all shook up, but I also want to find serenity at the core of things. Jesus will provide that, although I come with no illusions that I'll be comforted in the cozy sense that the word *comfort* has taken on.

THE QUESTION which I bring with me now is not the one we typically hear is the "great question" of Christianity: "How can I be saved?" We frequently are informed that Christianity is a "salvation" faith, that it is preoccupied with "eternal life," which for most seems to mean "getting to heaven and avoiding hell." In this regard, we are told, it differs from those wisdom traditions that ask other great questions, such as "How can I be enlightened?" and "How can I avoid suffering?"

However, I come to Jesus with the question that is the one shared by all faiths and philosophies: "How should I live my life?" It is, I dare to think, the question most of his first followers brought with them to his conferences. They were concerned primarily with their lives here and now. Salvation and eternal life are not unimportant issues, and they are certainly serious matters for the Christian to contemplate. But Jesus spoke more about the life we must live with God in this world than about any other subject, and this is especially noticeable in the Sermon on the Mount. Like it or not, if I desire absolute assurance of my life beyond this one, I must leave that to the grace, mercy, and work of Christ on my behalf. What's left to me is this: the question "How should I live?" It is, in fact, more crucial to me now than it ever was before. As the Bob Dylan song has it, "It's not dark yet, but it's getting there." And *I'm* getting there, and I'm closer to "there" now than I was just a moment ago. My days on earth grow shorter, and I've made a number of mistakes thus far. So, how should I live my life — from this time on to the very end? The next life I leave entirely to God, as I must.

This brings me to my personal history.

No true philosophy or theology can be disconnected from autobiography. Even the most abstract systems derive from somebody's subjective point of view. In one vital sense, all of us are self-centered: we can think and feel only from the center we call the "self." So, my personal history colors my perspective as I come to Jesus. The same is true for you.

I will comment very briefly on my personal history, then, before I invite you further to approach the mountain in my company. You may not want to come, so here's your opportunity to leave me behind and go up some other way. As I have already indicated, I've been around long enough to have garnered significant regrets and griefs in my life. Going up to listen again to Jesus engenders in me humility and shamefacedness.

What will I do, for example, when I — a divorced and remarried man — am confronted by Jesus' words about precisely these things? I know I will have to lay this aspect of my life before him. Divorce was something I never wanted, but there are numerous realities in one's life that one neither wants nor welcomes. What of the ambiguity of remarriage? My second marriage has been a great joy and solace to me. Can I bring that with me, and the experience of its goodness, and expect to have it pass the test of Jesus' words? I hope I can. I hope, if you carry a similar burden, that you can.

Besides that, I am a former priest. I left the priesthood, a life consecrated to the service of the church, because I could no longer offer that institution's hierarchy the sort of obedience ordained life entailed. I will only say that, more than anything else, it was the clerical sexual-abuse crisis that shook my confidence in the institutional church. I could no longer accept a functional role within a system I had come, sadly, to distrust profoundly. It demanded from me too great a faith in externals. I found I needed a faith that either sinks or swims in the currents of a lived life, one that has for its only foundation trust in God alone, a faith that is internal and visceral and intelligent. To echo Abraham Joshua Heschel, faith is not adherence to dogmas or definitions, but to the God that dogmas and definitions can only *indicate*. I think I can live with my decision to leave the priesthood, if only because it demanded faith in God to take that step. I can't say I regret the decision at all. But I can honestly say that it has caused others hurt and consternation, and maybe it has even shaken the faith of a few. Can I carry this baggage up the mountain, or even make the apparently audacious claim that I am a disciple? I think I can, but not without some hesitancy of conscience.

Those are two weights I carry as I come again to listen to Jesus. Perhaps you carry such things yourself. If you are my age, I suspect you do. How shall we approach Jesus with such things on our consciences?

I COME TO Jesus, then, as a modern-postmodern man. I step, as we all must, from our present world into his. I know that I will find perennial wisdom here. What belongs uniquely to his age and culture can be translated into mine. I believe that, or I wouldn't come to him once again.

I come again to the mountain, too, at a particular historical moment when religion is distrusted. As I've already noted, the church that bears his name faces a grave crisis of credibility. By the same token, Muslims have been compromised by the actions of their co-religionists who are bent on terrorism and murder in God's name. I mention these two faiths in particular, but all religious faiths are currently called into question because of the intolerance, violence, perversity, and fanaticism of some of their adherents. It has become almost a truism for some secular pundits and atheistic thinkers that religion is in and of itself dangerous to the peace of the world. Of course this is nonsense. The problems of humanity are not the result of religion; rather, religion is just one arena among many where the problems of humanity can be seen at work. But, because of the lofty claims made by all the great religions, the enormity of visible evil at work in them appears magnified.

Nevertheless, in a historical moment when the Roman Catholic Church looks morally discredited to many, and adherence to

Islam appears to its despisers to be only an excuse for bloody-mindedness, whether these are unjust caricatures or not, it is important for us to go back to the sources of faith and listen intelligently to them once again. If we believe, we must constantly measure what it is we believe against the best standards set for our belief. It's important that each person does this for himself or herself. We can't blame the impersonal face of a "religion" or of an "institution." Faith is a personal quality, not an impersonal one — indeed, it is a *human* and primarily *individual* one. No one else, and certainly no institution, can believe for me or for you.

It's not sufficient any longer to ask what the church says or doesn't say, as if external religious authority can be trusted to have it all together infallibly. It may provide a touchstone, certainly; but the belief itself belongs to us. Besides, Jesus himself is the model for taking precisely this tack. We must internalize our faith, not let an institution simply hand us a creed and ask us to sign at the bottom. So, it is important for the Christian disciple regularly to go straight back to Jesus. If I am at all a person with even a shred of self-reliance (in the best sense) and a working mind, I can go and sit quietly before him, and expect to receive what I most need directly from that pristine source.

AND WHAT I most need now is simple guidance in living my life. In this regard, I approach his words as "everyman" to some extent. I would like my approach in these pages to be as minimalist in theory as I can make it. Again, I will cut theological reasoning and doctrinal concepts to the bare bones. I welcome any fellow travelers who are not decided Christians, and who wish nonetheless to join me, to come along. Elsewhere I have written specifically for Christians, but here I write for both Christians and non-Christians. This is not a book of doctrinal argument, defending this or that theological position, this or that church; it is simply sitting before Jesus, asking him about living life, listening to him, and taking notes. This may be the simplest form of prayer as well, since prayer is first and foremost openness, questioning, and hearing. Stillness and listening.

I believe that this "everyman" approach to the Sermon on the Mount is justified. It is open to hearing Jesus' words with a sort of freshness, not entirely unlike the openness of those who listened to Jesus originally. They came without preconceived notions about him. Perhaps they had seen his healing work, or at least had heard of it. They came to him for healing, on the one hand, showing their primary concern for their worldly lives. On the other hand, they came to him for his words. "And when Jesus finished these sayings, the crowds were astonished at his teaching, for he taught them as one who had authority, and not as their scribes" (Matt. 7:28-29). John's Gospel even tells how some who had been sent to place Jesus under arrest testified to the power of his words instead: "No man ever spoke like this man!" (John 7:46).

It seems certain, then, that it was as a teacher that Jesus made his greatest impact on his disciples. I would argue that the same holds true today. If people — whether disaffected from belief or unknowledgeable about it — are to become re-acquainted with Jesus now, it won't be on the grounds of doctrines about him or the claims of even the oldest churches. Such things may have their value in time for those who rediscover Jesus. But, first and foremost, they must listen to his words again. Becoming his disciple — a "learner" — means hearing him and weighing his words. Some may hear and weigh, and never become Christian disciples. But at least they won't easily confuse him with the worst exemplars of those who profess faith in him, or even for the merely poor ones.

Regarding that last point, I will make a brief aside. I have no intention whatever of denying the relative importance of either the historical church (meaning, correctly, the "assembly" of all God's people), or the other books of the Bible. The church and its Bible have guarded, contextualized, and carried on the heritage and tradition of Israel and "the method and secret and temper of Jesus" (as Matthew Arnold put it). Nonetheless, permit me two stories and an observation by Kurt Vonnegut ("Of all people!" you may think).

The first story was recounted to me by a friend. I cannot vouch firsthand for the accuracy of what my friend said he heard, but I know him well enough to believe he heard it correctly. He was listening to a fundamentalist Protestant televangelist one morning, mesmerized by the performance on the screen, but increasingly unsettled by the working up of both the preacher and his audience as the former's sermon turned more and more into a rant. As the sweat poured and the face of the preacher grew purple with passion, he exclaimed, Bible in hand: "I get sick and tired of 'nice' people who say to me, when I preach hard biblical truths, 'Yes, preacher, but what would Jesus do? What would Jesus say?' *Well, I tell them, I don't care what Jesus would say — what does the Bible say?*"

I doubt the poor preacher meant to say such a thing. He was caught up in the moment and whipped up by his own rhetoric. Such an emotionally wrought condition can lead to idiotic words and frightful actions. That said, what he shouted out was an unintentional blasphemy.

The other story is one I experienced firsthand. It occurred at a roundtable discussion between a dozen or so Catholic priests. A rather sticky point of canon law was being debated regarding a local pastoral matter concerning two civilly married Catholic laypersons — married, that is, without benefit of clergy, and who were now as a result being barred from communion. One priest, obviously troubled by some of the tough "rule of law" viewpoints expressed by a few of his colleagues, brought up the same naïve question so detested by the preacher above: "What would Jesus do?" At this point, another, somewhat younger priest, squirming in his chair with evident agitation, blurted out in response one of the most inadvertently humorous lines I have ever heard uttered by a clergyman (and, frankly, I've heard a few): *"Jesus would have obeyed the church!"* Humorous, yes (and I broke out laughing, I confess, much to this young priest's consternation); but, sadly, he meant it. Unlike the blasphemous words of the apoplectic Protestant preacher above, what the priest said was merely foolish. In retrospect, he might have wanted to kick himself.

Such offhanded declarations as these two examples provide should concern those of us who want to see Jesus rightly presented and understood. They reveal attitudes that lurk just under the surface among Christians of all sorts. They expose how Jesus is actually often regarded by many of his supposed followers. For some, it is the Bible that is worshiped and given pride of place, even above Jesus. For others, it is the church's institutional sacramental or hierarchical power that stands above him. In both cases, Jesus has ceased to be taken seriously in his own right.

On to the observation of Kurt Vonnegut, then. In a May 2004 article for "In These Times" (which can be found online), Vonnegut wrote the following:

> For some reason, the most vocal Christians among us never mention the Beatitudes. But, often with tears in their eyes, they demand that the Ten Commandments be posted in public buildings. And of course that's Moses, not Jesus. I haven't heard one of them demand that the Sermon on the Mount, the Beatitudes, be posted anywhere.
>
> "Blessed are the merciful" in a courtroom? "Blessed are the peacemakers" in the Pentagon? Give me a break!

Vonnegut, it seems to me needless to say, got it right. Either we follow Jesus, or we do not — and this will be the theme of this entire book, really. Following the Ten Commandments is not the same as following Jesus, as he himself indicated in the Sermon on the Mount (the latter is in some ways — not to make too fine a point on it — more demanding than the Decalogue). If one seeks to follow Jesus, then the words of Jesus must stand above church, Bible, and Ten Commandments. Indeed, they stand above the rest of the New Testament, the greatest theologians, the most convincing and elegant theological systems, the creeds and formulas, confessions and dogmas, and everything else ecclesiastical or religious or secular. That's the "cost of discipleship," the "taking up of the cross," and so forth. If we don't honor Jesus' words above all else, then the rest of the church's furniture and formularies aren't really worth a dime.

IN WRITING what I have above about the sayings of Jesus as recorded in the Gospels, I wish to add that I am aware of the questions and scholarly difficulties surrounding them. What can be taken as authentic, and what must be qualified? All four of the Gospels are highly edited works, with differing emphases and audiences. There are numerous differences between them, including differences of what, where, and when Jesus said this, that, or the other thing. All four were committed to writing a generation or two after his ministry's completion, and were based on oral traditions. Further, Jesus himself taught in Aramaic, but our Gospels were all originally written in Greek, the *lingua franca* of the time. Other problems could be listed, but let me assume that you get the drift and leave it there.

I don't wish to trivialize any of these matters; but I also don't wish to exaggerate them, as some have done. Chances are good that we have the basic teachings of Jesus pretty well intact. The Sermon on the Mount is one place where we can believe that we have a sustained body of authentic teaching from Jesus, though not without editing and adaptation. However, this book is not a work of scholarly research or, worse, scholarly nitpicking. It is, rather, a personal reflection on the sources we actually have, and not on whatever we might wish we had instead. (For those interested in the difficulties surrounding Jesus' words and my own thinking about them, see Appendix 1. The two appendices, I should mention, are more directly addressed to a specifically Christian readership than is the body of this book.)

A final comment regarding the English translation I have used throughout the book may be in order. It is the Revised Standard Version. My own personal preference when reading the Bible in English has always been the King James Version. As far as I'm concerned, no other translation can match its sublimity, cadences, and majesty. It is, without doubt, always and ever shall be quite simply *The English Bible*. But, having admitted my own bias, I also know that the KJV has been surpassed in accuracy of translation by later versions and, further, that its language is archaic for modern readers. So, for teaching, I've long settled on the Revised Standard Version as a compromise. To be completely honest, I don't care for most modern translations. I'm a nitpicker, I'm stodgy, I'm rapidly becoming archaic myself, and all these newfangled translations are coming out faster than I can keep up with them. So it's the RSV I've settled on here, because I've used it for many years and know it well — as many readers will too.

So, please join me as I come back to the Sermon on the Mount. Together let us try to hear Jesus afresh.

2

Setting the Context of the Sermon

MATTHEW 4:17–5:2

17From that time Jesus began to preach, saying, "Repent, for the kingdom of heaven is at hand." 18As he walked by the Sea of Galilee, he saw two brothers, Simon who is called Peter and Andrew his brother, casting a net into the sea; for they were fishermen. 19And he said to them, "Follow me, and I will make you fishers of men." 20Immediately they left their nets and followed him. 21And going on from there he saw two other brothers, James the son of Zebedee and John his brother, in the boat with Zebedee their father, mending their nets, and he called them. 22Immediately they left the boat and their father, and followed him. 23And he went about all Galilee, teaching in their synagogues and preaching the gospel of the kingdom and healing every disease and every infirmity among the people. 24So his fame spread throughout all Syria, and they brought him all the sick, those afflicted with various diseases and pains, demoniacs, epileptics, and paralytics, and he healed them. 25And great crowds followed him from Galilee and the Decapolis and Jerusalem and Judea and from beyond the Jordan. 5:1Seeing the crowds, he

*went up on the mountain, and when he sat down his disciples
came to him. ²And he opened his mouth and taught them....*

B efore we come to the mountain where Jesus gave his teaching, Matthew provides us with some details about the stir-
ring context in which it was delivered. We are given the following
information:

1. Following his baptism by John the Baptist, Jesus began to proclaim his message.
2. He gathered about him his first disciples.
3. They followed him, observing his ministry of healing.
4. As a result, his fame spread, and great crowds gathered to see
   and hear him. These crowds included not only his fellow Galilean northerners, but also Judeans from the south, and possibly even non-Jews. (Galilee was especially known for the diver-
   sity of peoples settled there; and the mention of Syria, the
   Decapolis, and "beyond the Jordan" may all suggest that his
   popularity and renown went even beyond strictly Jewish
   boundaries.)
5. Seeing the crowds his acts had drawn to him, he ascended a
   mountain, sat down (the traditional teaching posture in the
   East), and taught his disciples, passing along his wisdom first
   of all to them.

This is the scene we now approach, and I think it's necessary
for us to re-examine it. It is a familiar scene to many of us: Jesus
preaching the kingdom, healing the multitudes, and teaching.
These are all pictures we have in our minds from Sunday school,
perhaps, or stained-glass windows, or picture Bibles, or our own
imaginations. It's easy to go quickly by all these details, as perhaps we do with the imagery of Christmas and Easter each year,
and not stop to look and listen more closely. Nor will I pause to
dwell on every aspect of the text here. But I wish to tease out

those few things which have particularly struck me in my rereading of the passage.

The first is Jesus' great proclamation: "Repent, for the kingdom of heaven is at hand."

The Greek word "repent" literally means "change your minds" or "thoughts" or "thinking" *(metanoeite)*. It has to do with our inner selves, our thoughts, feelings, minds, attitudes, and so on. Too often we assume that the word "repent" is a word of judgment or condemnation. The cartoon image of a sandaled and robed man with a long white beard, bearing a placard with that exclamatory word on it and marching down a city sidewalk annoying the passersby, comes to mind. Perhaps we think "repentance" has to do with fiery retribution, an approaching apocalypse, doom and gloom and an angry God.

It means no such thing, however.

It means, in this context, to "change the way you live your life," and the way we live our lives has everything to do with the way we think about life in general. Something profound must change within the depths of our selves. Our thoughts must be altered.

Further, the word is in the imperative tense. That simply means that it is a command, an exclamation, an alarm. It has the force of "Wake up!" or "Run!" It's not a suggestion, in other words. It is a bracing red alert. The fact that it is an imperative means, of course, that we are urged strongly to do something. Jesus expects us to act, to be pragmatic, to exert ourselves. There is nothing passive in this; Jesus affirms our autonomy and our ability to stand up for ourselves.

Nor is this exclamation of Jesus a threat. It is described as "gospel" (v. 23) — that is to say, "good news." It is a word of hope: "Get ready — something very good has arrived!"

That also means that neither is "the kingdom of heaven" being "at hand" a threat. Matthew frequently uses the term "the kingdom of heaven" (or, more literally, "the heavens") where the other Gospels use "the kingdom of God." This is likely because he prefers, in pious Jewish fashion, not to use the word "God" too often. "God" is not a title to be used casually or lightly. One approaches it and the One it signifies with caution and awe. So he replaces it with "heaven" more often than not.

When Jesus says that "the kingdom of heaven is at hand," he is saying that it is "near" or — more to the point — it is here, right under our noses, within reach. It means, as he says to the Pharisees in Luke 17:20-21, that "the kingdom of God is within you" or "within your grasp [if you'll just reach for it]." Similarly, in the Gospel of Thomas, Jesus says, "The kingdom is inside of you, and it is outside of you" (logion 2), and "The kingdom of the Father is spread out upon the earth, and men do not see it" (logion 113). Although not within the canon, these apocryphal words nonetheless accord well with the four biblical Gospels concerning the nature of God's "kingdom." The kingdom is somehow present now and within reach. Again, this is a message not of threat, but of hope.

This leaves us with two important questions, and we often believe we possess adequate answers for them already. In fact, however, we may need to dispense with any notion that we have sure-fire answers to them. The two questions are these: First, quite simply, what does Jesus mean by "kingdom"? And, second, what does this mean for you and me? The Sermon on the Mount will indeed hang on a suitable understanding of what is meant by this phrase ("the kingdom of heaven" or "the kingdom of God"), and so we must get it as right as we can.

To ANSWER the first question, we must say that Jesus' use of the word "kingdom" to refer to his program was potentially inflammatory in the world in which he preached it. To see how provocative it was, one need only consider the execution of Jesus, and the derisive reason given — nailed above his head — for that terrible act: "This is Jesus the King of the Jews" (Matt. 27:37). There was only one recognized "kingdom" *(basileia)* in Roman Palestine, one which had been imposed with violence and was enforced with all the power of self-legitimating authority, and that was the Roman "empire" *(basileia)*. The fact that Jesus announced the arrival of another "kingdom" in a province governed by Rome, under the very nose of the Roman governor, so to speak, was daring, to say the least. The term was familiar to the Jewish people, derived as it was from both scriptural and apocryphal prophecies, associated with the advent of Israel's "Messiah" (Israel's expected, true "anointed" king, in other words, and not the Gentile emperor in Rome), who would restore the kingdom of David — the kingdom of God — to the Jewish people. As commonly hoped for, God's warrior-king would crush the Gentiles' lord and give the land back to his own people.

What Jesus did with the word "kingdom" was something else entirely. Just as he redefined such concepts as "Messiah" through his life and character, so he redefined not only the Romans' idea of "kingdom," but also Israel's. He took this term, removed its content, and replaced it with new content and meaning. No longer was the kingdom of God a restoration of the dynasty of David, an Eastern potentate with his force of arms, won at the expense of bloodshed and war. Nor was it a kingdom — a *basileia* — even remotely similar to that of Rome. Indeed, the kingdom Jesus said he came to proclaim was a kingdom where children come first and the first come last, where hierarchy is inverted so that the poor and slaves are given dignity, where all are brothers and sisters, and so on. The term "kingdom of heaven" appears to be used almost ironically by Jesus, if it wasn't irony outright. At any rate, it no longer meant what the world thought of when it thought of a "kingdom." To the world — Jewish or Gentile — it could look only like an "un-kingdom," which was precisely the point. God's empire, in other words, was the opposite of the world's, and most particularly of Rome's. (It is a further and deeply sad irony that Jesus' inversion was itself later inverted by the Roman emperor Constantine and his "heirs" — both political and ecclesiastical —

so that "the kingdom of heaven" was corrupted into the worldly "Christendom." But I'm not so much interested here in the historical perversion of Jesus' message as I am in seeking to rediscover the original for ourselves.)

There are three characteristics of the kingdom of heaven, as Jesus presents it. The first two we have already touched upon. First of all, the kingdom is *present*. It is not a matter of something that lies only in some as yet unrealized future. But, if it is present, how is its presence to be understood?

Second, the kingdom is, or will be, *everywhere;* and Jesus describes it (as we shall see) as spreading and growing. In what sense is it everywhere if, as the Gospel of Thomas has it, "men do not see it"? Surely, as the Sermon on the Mount will make very clear, it is meant to be seen. How will it be visible everywhere, then?

The first and second characteristics raise questions for which the third characteristic suggests answers. Third, then, the kingdom of heaven is an internal reality that becomes visible in the way people's lives are actually lived. It is both mystical and pragmatic. It begins as a message, becomes a way of life, and ultimately — through the lives of those who try to live it — becomes an influence in the world. The apostle Paul understood Jesus' intention perfectly well when he wrote, "For the kingdom of God is not food and drink [that is to say, it is not a matter of trifling externals] but righteousness and peace and joy in the Holy Spirit" (Rom. 14:17). In other words, it is a matter of internal character and practical life.

Jesus' message is about a way of life, a way of being and thinking and doing. It guides both actions and reactions. It finds its strength in an inner life, and the peace and compassion that that interior discipline engenders are meant to be visible to others. The kingdom of the Romans was external, imposed from above, ruled from the top down, hierarchical, militant, cruel, legalistic, moralistic, and oppressive. The kingdom of heaven, in contrast, is internal (and thus hidden from plain sight), received through a listening ear, guided from within, egalitarian, pacifistic, kind, generous, loving, and freeing. It is an invisible empire, one in which God flows through the veins and lives of human beings, and reaches ever further and further out through them to others. The kingdom of Rome and all other worldly powers are merely organizations. The kingdom of heaven is, if lived rightly, organic and an organism. It is personal, multifaceted, and — to the frustration of all would-be supreme organizers of it, both ecclesiastical and political — ultimately guided by no single organizing power. It moves through individuals, binds them into relationships, and passes on in some indefinable way from generation to generation. It has never been fully harnessed, and no church or nation can control its internal life. It remains, it would seem, working as it does from within the human person, what we might well think of as *God's* domain.

So it is that we should think "way of life" whenever we hear the terms "kingdom of heaven" and "kingdom of God." Indeed, as the book of Acts informs us, the first followers of Jesus were simply said to be followers of "the Way."

THE SECOND question posed for us was this pragmatic one: What does all this mean for you and me? In the pages that follow, we turn our attention to the words of Jesus in the Sermon on the Mount and seek answers to this question in simple, direct, and practical terms. If we want to follow this "way" ourselves, how are we to hear these words and take them in?

Two caveats might be worth addressing here briefly, though we will come back to them again and again, if in less explicit fashion.

First, it has often been stated that the Sermon on the Mount is too difficult an ideal to follow, that it proposes an unrealistic standard of behavior that is practicably unattainable. Those who say such things are, of course, merely pointing out that it is *difficult,* and it is; but they fail to make a case that it is impossible. In *What's Wrong with the World,* G. K. Chesterton famously wrote that "the Christian ideal has not been tried and found wanting; it has been found difficult and left untried." He may have been exaggerating a bit in the other direction, but basically he was right. If we make the mistake, for example, of thinking that such concepts as "love," "forgiveness," and "not judging others" are rooted in our feelings, and not in our actions (or, sometimes, our *non-actions*), we will indeed become frustrated, perhaps feel guilty of failure, and maybe even give up entirely on attempting "the impossible." But Jesus, as we will see, is not addressing our *feelings* at all — not even the transformation of our feelings. He is giving practical guidance. And this is why we are approaching him now — for just that sort of instruction.

It will always be wise for us not to chalk up our failures, too. We will fall short. When we do, we get back up, brush ourselves off, and get back on the way. No one — least of all Jesus — expects us to be "perfect"; and when he does tell us to "be perfect" in the Sermon on the Mount (5:48), it does not mean "perfect" in the way we often mistakenly take this word in this context to mean. At any rate, we are beginners each and every day. We should heed the advice of Shunryu Suzuki. In *Zen Mind, Beginner's Mind,* he said, "The goal of practice is always to keep our beginner's mind. . . . When we have no thought of achievement, no thought of self, we are true beginners. Then we can really learn something. The beginner's mind is the mind of compassion." If one can learn patience with oneself, one can learn, perhaps, to have compassion and non-judgment towards others. Suzuki's words regarding Zen practice are applicable to us in our desire to follow Jesus' Way.

But the second caveat is a caution that we should not take Jesus' words too lightly, either. As we shall see, they are intimately connected with an idea of judgment. They are not, despite their often beautiful phrases, sentimental or merely inspirational in tone. They are not greeting-card sentiments. The Sermon on the

Mount concludes with a warning, and therefore it ends on a note of urgency. We are truly meant to work and apply ourselves to this way, to life in this kingdom. (In Appendix 2 I have provided an explanation — as I understand it — of the overall role of judgment in Matthew's Gospel.) Jesus cautions us against hearing only, but not doing (7:24-27). This is meant not to discourage us, but to bring before our minds the weightiness of his teachings. They are not given casually or carelessly.

With these things in mind, we come to Jesus, who is seated in the style of the Eastern sage. He instructs us.

3

What Jesus' Beatitudes Mean for Our Discipleship

—⟡—

5:2And he opened his mouth and taught them, saying:
3"Blessed are the poor in spirit, for theirs is the kingdom of heaven.
4"Blessed are those who mourn, for they shall be comforted.
5"Blessed are the meek, for they shall inherit the earth.
6"Blessed are those who hunger and thirst for righteousness, for they shall be satisfied.
7"Blessed are the merciful, for they shall obtain mercy.
8"Blessed are the pure in heart, for they shall see God.
9"Blessed are the peacemakers, for they shall be called sons of God.
10"Blessed are those who are persecuted for righteousness' sake, for theirs is the kingdom of heaven.
11"Blessed are you when men revile you and persecute you and utter all kinds of evil against you falsely on my account.
12Rejoice and be glad, for your reward is great in heaven, for so men persecuted the prophets who were before you."

The first words of Jesus that we hear are a series of blessings, or benedictions — that is to say, "words bestowing well-being."

Each blessing has three parts: first, the pronouncement of *blessing* itself; second, an element of *character*, or a consequence for exhibiting such character, that obtains Jesus' blessing; and third, the *promise* that Jesus attaches to each of his blessings. Blessing, character, promise. If we are hoping to understand the qualities that describe those who are in the kingdom of heaven — that is to say, those who endeavor to follow Jesus' way — then here is the place to start. With these nine pronouncements of beatitude in Matthew's account, Jesus shows us what these qualities are.

First, what is meant by "blessed"? Some translations render the Greek word for "blessed" *(makarioi)* as "happy." In his book *The Ladder of the Beatitudes,* Jim Forest convincingly shows why the word "happy" is inadequate as a translation, and why the original is better rendered "blessed" in English. I refer the reader to this fine book, which presents the Beatitudes as a series of steps, with each next step resting on the preceding one. Among Forest's arguments against translating the Greek word as "happy," he points out that it carries with it a sort of intimation of immortality — it means a type of joy that transcends mere "happiness" (the latter English word suggests whatever may "happen" to one by chance). Blessedness is fuller than transitory pleasure or good feelings. It is stable and permanent, not dependent on any "happenstance," and it relates to a life greater and richer than a merely mundane one.

A benediction also represents the pronouncement of a judgment, in this case one that will be realized in the future. It corresponds to this: "Come, O blessed of my Father, inherit the kingdom prepared for you from the foundation of the world" (Matt. 25:34). In succinct fashion the word "blessed" says, in effect, that what one becomes and does in the here and now has lasting consequences. One of those consequences can be blessedness (thus receiving a "bene-diction," meaning "good word"); and the contrary would be a condition of "woe" (receiving a corresponding "male-diction," a "bad word"). In Luke's Gospel, Jesus gives not only a series of benedictions but also a parallel set of maledictions (Luke 6:20-26). Here we will stick with Matthew's version, however, except to note that every benediction infers an analogous, even if left unsaid, malediction. A judgment is thus implied here at the outset, but at the very end of the Sermon on the Mount it will be made explicit.

The blessings of Jesus have to do with character, and character has to do with both what one is becoming and what one is putting into practice. It has to do with the inner life and the outer one. It draws us to both interiority and right external conduct, contemplation and action, mysticism and pragmatism. Neither end of the pole is neglected; both the inner and the outer aspects of the person are embraced in the simple words of Jesus. There is no hint of the medieval notion that contemplation is superior to action, or the modern idea that action leaves no time for a contemplative inner life. The first seven of the Beatitudes present us with an element of character. The last two blessings speak of the possible consequences of living out that character in a world that lives according to other, very different principles.

Let's begin by discussing the *elements* that are blessed.

THE FIRST benediction is for "the poor in spirit." In Luke's version, Jesus says only, "Blessed are you poor" (Luke 6:20). In Matthew's version, this quality is taken to the very depths of the human heart and mind — into "the spirit." Behind this deepening of blessing "the poor" to "the poor in spirit" may lie such passages as Isaiah 66:2b, in which God says, "But this is the man to whom I will look, he that is humble and contrite in spirit, and trembles at my word." It is an interior quality of openness and emptiness, not full of oneself. It corresponds to the fourth beatitude — "hungering and thirsting for righteousness." In fact, "poverty in spirit" may well include in itself all the other elements of character blessed by Jesus. That the promise attached to it is that those who are poor in spirit will possess the full richness of the kingdom sug-

ROIZOI 03251

gests that this beatitude (like the eighth beatitude) is inclusive of the other blessings and their promises.

To be "poor in spirit" means that we realize that we all depend on others, on the creation around us, and ultimately on God. We must depend on all these merely to exist, merely to get by each day. Every breath we take is a testimony to dependence. No one is self-sufficient; and independence is quite literally impossible. Everyone is essentially in need every day. We begin and end in need, not with sufficiency, efficiency, or fullness. This is, for one thing, the profound realization that should lead us to the sort of prayer that Jesus will teach us later in the Sermon (6:5-15).

"Poverty in spirit" as an ideal is also a warning against materialism, the accumulation of riches and goods, and the all-too-easy ignoring of others' needs. If we follow Jesus, we are not free to look the other way when confronted with evident need. Obviously, none of us can deal with the overwhelming demands that surround us daily. But we can attend to some — volunteer to assist at soup kitchens or the local Salvation Army outlet, or whatever is at hand. We can give out of our pockets, learn to be generous, and — most essential of all — seek detachment where material things are concerned. Detachment is the inner quality we must strive to acquire. We must learn to be satisfied with what we have.

Poverty in spirit is not, however, a glorification of poverty. Francis of Assisi is someone I admire greatly, but he died in his mid-forties from extreme asceticism resulting in malnourishment (as forensic work on his remains has indicated). That is no ideal for anybody, even if we see in him other ideals to emulate. Nor does Jesus call us to such life-denying self-punishment. Asceticism as self-discipline is a fine thing — saying no to ourselves and not indulging our every whim is a sign of maturity and self-control. But asceticism as a perverse hatred of one's supposedly sinful body (the body is good, and so are food, drink, marriage, sex, children, and so on), or as an elevation of suffering as a good thing (it isn't), or as a way to win God's affection (it doesn't win any such thing, or need to) — these are things to be resisted. They have twisted the lives of countless Christians down the centuries and find no support from Jesus.

Self-denial in Jesus' teachings simply means putting God's kingdom first, and — as we will see — enduring the possible consequences for living according to its ways within the context of a hostile world order. Self-denial does not mean self-flagellation or a "Uriah Heep" type of humility.

Suffering is likewise never good in and of itself. The endurance we may need to exhibit when we suffer is a good quality to have; but Jesus never exalts suffering as anything more than suffering — pain is an evil thing, which even Jesus dreaded (Matt. 26:36-42). Self-inflicted suffering has no role to play in our salvation or our repentance.

THE SECOND beatitude is for "those who mourn." The promise is that "they shall be comforted," and that tells us something about what sort of mourning Jesus means. The word "comforted" *(paraklethesontai)* refers to being strengthened or fortified. It may mean "mourning" for one's sins, as some have suggested, but that is doubtful. It more likely refers to the sort of sorrow we will have in this life — everything from melancholy to grief. This world will not be "all sunshine" (as the saccharine words of Father Faber's old hymn puts it), not even for those who follow the way of Jesus. There will be suffering, death, and bad things we cannot understand. Jesus is a realist. He was never a dreamer, disconnected from the real world, as some have misrepresented him. He didn't have his head in the clouds. Nonetheless, in the midst of troubles, sorrows, depression, and grief, strength is at hand. As we shall see, it comes from God; but it comes from God through both an inner discipline and a community of like-minded disciples.

NEXT IS THE blessing of "the meek." Here we might do better to translate the word as "gentle" or even "not easily angered." "Meekness" unfortunately carries with it the connotation of "weakness," and that is not at all the meaning of Jesus. If this blessing is, as appears to be the case, an echo of Psalm 37:11 ("But the meek shall possess the land"), then Jesus' meaning is something akin to "non-violence." Psalm 37:8-9 says, "Refrain from anger, and forsake wrath! Fret not yourself; it tends only to evil. For the wicked shall be cut off; but those who wait for the LORD shall possess the land." In other words, do not seek to retaliate with hostility against those who mistreat you, no matter how you feel about it, but leave justice to God. Jesus will pick up this line of thought later in the Sermon, but here he touches on the theme of non-retaliation, standing one's ground and turning the other cheek, not striking back or resorting to violence.

Revenge and acting out of anger against an injustice are rejected. This involves yet another inner discipline. If poverty in spirit entails detachment from outward material things, gentleness entails detachment from being blown about by our inner passions — even those which we think we can justify as "right." "Inheriting the earth" has been expanded in the context of the Beatitudes to mean, once again, inheriting the kingdom in its fullness.

THEN COMES the blessing of "those who hunger and thirst for righteousness." "They shall be," says Jesus, "satisfied." Following upon the previous beatitude, this one also reminds us to leave justice in the capable hands of God. "Fret not yourself; it tends only to evil." Our enforcement of justice, if it is done violently, angrily, loudly, stridently, or without gentleness, will only create a new injustice in place of the old. Every revolution has only replaced one set of injustices and inequities with another. We fool ourselves in believing that wrathful, fist-pumping, angry rhetoric and behavior can produce anything but more troubles and misery. They always have backfired and always will. Real change comes through those who "hunger and thirst for righteousness," and are satisfied when they implement it through gentleness and loving action. There is nothing weak in this. It takes patience, endurance, and strength. Anger and violence are the methods of the puerile and those lacking in self-control.

"THE MERCIFUL," says Jesus next, "shall obtain mercy." It is the correlate of "meekness" above; but whereas meekness is reactive, mercy is proactive. It reaches out. It sees a need (sickness, imprisonment, hunger, thirst, or any other calamity), and it acts. Jesus' paramount parable in Matthew is that of 25:31-46, which connects the judgment of each of us to precisely this characteristic. (See Appendix 2 for a fuller discussion of this parable and its meaning for us.)

"BLESSED ARE the pure in heart" indicates inward cleansing. It isn't, of course, that anyone is born with such purity of heart, but that one works at having it. It is, as many commentators have noted, a *singleness* of intention that is meant here, a focus on what is most necessary and pursuing it. Jesus will come back to this theme later in the Sermon (6:22-24). The promise attached to this blessing is that those who have made their interior lives central to their activities — have guarded themselves from distractions and from thoughts and images that contaminate the mind and memory — "shall see God." That is to say, cleansed inwardly from false concepts and false "gods," they shall somehow perceive that which is beyond all concepts, know what is ultimate and true. They will learn to "see" what is essentially invisible through and within the creation that is visible.

The one who seeks shall find, and God is the One that sums up all that is good, righteous, real, and eternal — in other words, all that is to be sought in all things. Jesus referred to God as his Father, and more intimately as his "Abba" ("Papa"). He could look out over creation, and, despite the miseries he daily confronted, still see the beauty and essential goodness of the earth and heavens, and perceive in them the Father from whom all came. He could feel "at home" in the creation, not an alien within it, aware of the constant and living One at work through what is ever-changing in nature's cycles of birth and death and rebirth. So alert to these things was he that they provided the natural imagery of his parables. He could thus "see God"; and his promise to "the pure in heart" is that they could, too, if they purified their minds.

"THE PEACEMAKERS" whom Jesus next blesses are those who bring about reconciliation and harmony among persons and factions. Jesus regarded his disciples as a "family" of "brothers and sisters." "You are all brethren," he says, for instance, in Matthew 23:8. Peacemakers are those who maintain this outlook in the community of disciples, who insist upon it, and promote it urgently. Disunity, anger, bitterness, backbiting, gossip, and all the other things that break down relationships, create suspicion, keep people from talking to each other, and form cliques are all to be disowned and uprooted by peacemakers. And since all these blessed characteristics are meant to describe us all, at least ideally, and not just a select group within the circle of disciples, then we are *all* called to be such peacemakers. Intolerance itself is not to be tolerated, hatred is to be hated, and disunity is to be cut off.

Such workers for the sake of peace are promised a title that is exalted indeed. It is one used for Jesus himself ("Son of God" and just "the Son," when used in regard to Jesus, turn up in Matthew in 4:3, 6; 8:29; 11:27; 14:33; 24:36; 26:63-64; 27:54; and 28:19). The inference is that there is something quite Jesus-like about the actions of peacemakers, and thus they can share a title which is normally attached to him whenever it is used in the singular.

By extension, of course, "peacemakers" are also those who oppose conflict of any kind, war included. Jesus intended his disciples to influence nations and peoples, to be "the salt of the earth" and "the light of the world" (verses 13-14 below). In keeping with that expectation, no follower of Jesus is given license to justify the often alleged "need" for this or that war. No war is in fact needful or good. War is always the infliction of an unnecessary evil.

Later in Matthew's Gospel, Jesus speaks directly to his followers regarding the mistaken sentiment that there is ever a right time to wield the sword — even to protect him when the soldiers come to arrest him in Gethsemane — by saying that it is not permitted for them: "Put your sword back into its place; for all who take the sword will perish by the sword" (Matt. 26:52). The earliest generations of Christians took this to its logical conclusion, which — tragically for the credibility of Christianity in the eyes of many — later Christians compromised. No baptized disciple during the first three centuries of Christian history was supposed to be either a soldier or a magistrate. Either one did things the world's way, or one did things Jesus' way. Intentionally distancing oneself from legal and military service to the world was one of the hard choices one was expected to make when choosing citizenship in the kingdom of heaven. Is it any wonder, then, that early Christians were soon distrusted and persecuted by the authorities of the Roman Empire?

Peacemaking means working for other solutions in the affairs of the world than that of resorting to hostilities. The follower of Jesus is a practitioner and promoter of nonviolence, and normally should be uncooperative with every form of a nation's "war effort." If the cost to oneself is to be accused of lack of patriotism, so be it. Following Jesus means choosing his way without concession.

AND THIS brings us quite logically enough to the two concluding beatitudes.

Both have to do with persecution, but in the Greek text there is a difference of grammatical tense between them, and thus a difference in sense. The eighth blessing is upon those who have undergone persecution and carry the marks of it. "Theirs," says Jesus once again, "is the kingdom of heaven." Some past tribulation is referred to here. It's possible that Matthew put these words in Jesus' mouth, indicating possibly a later condition of persecution for his own contemporary community of disciples. Conceivably, for the same reason, he might have changed a present tense used by Jesus originally to the perfect participle passive (a tense which indicates a past action with ongoing repercussions in the present). Or perhaps Jesus is referring to the past ordeals of "the prophets who were before you" (v. 12). Whatever the reason for it, the eighth blessing as it stands indicates that persecution has already left its wounds on those who have sought to live "for righteousness' sake." Since "righteousness" means precisely the way of Jesus itself, a way of life lived as the Sermon on the Mount delineates it, they have suffered for living in accordance with that.

Jesus' promise to them is identical with his first promise: they shall inherit the kingdom. Bringing this full circle, so to speak, Jesus is saying that the characteristics he has blessed are those that offend the sensibilities of the world's powers; but that those persons who follow his alternative, subversive, and radical way will live as members of God's own good and eternal empire.

THE NINTH and final blessing carries the eighth a step further. If those who have already been persecuted have the promise of the kingdom, then, "you," too, will be blessed if you should suffer for the same righteousness. "*Your* reward also is great in [the kingdom of] heaven." This is an encouragement, of course, for us to stick to the way, even if we are "reviled," "persecuted," and "falsely accused" for doing so.

THUS THE FIRST twelve verses of the Sermon on the Mount present us with characteristics that Jesus will flesh out more fully in the remainder of this mountain discourse. The Beatitudes give us the contours of what the disciple is meant to grow into over the course of living life as Jesus' follower. The promises attached to each blessing are an incentive to continue on that course without compromise.

The warning at the end of the nine blessings, though, is purely realistic. Jesus was, after all, subverting the contemporary concept of "empire" itself; he was inverting the ideals considered so manly and virile in the Roman world. There is not one distinctively Roman virtue that he affirms. Gone is any praise of "justifiable" war and conquest (a theme lauded in Roman imperialism and glorified in its monuments and art); gone is any praise of a stoical and impassive stance in the face of suffering; gone is the honoring of the strong and the despising of the weak; gone is any congratulation for those who amass wealth or receive commendation for propping up an authoritarian system. In short, Jesus' values are not those of the world in which he lived. Nor are they those of the world today, no matter how much public lip service has been accorded them historically since the time of Constantine. Once again, in those words of Kurt Vonnegut which I quoted in the first chapter, "'Blessed are the merciful' in a courtroom? 'Blessed are the peacemakers' in the Pentagon? Give me a break!"

Jesus praises interior poverty (the knowledge of one's own emptiness and need), a realism (in place of escapism) that sees things clearly and knows there are many things to be mourned in an imperfect world, gentleness with all persons and all creation, a longing for true righteousness, mercy (instead of mere, lackluster fairness), inner cleansing from all false "gods" and misleading concepts and polluting images, nonviolence and pro-active peacemaking, and the willingness to suffer for these things in a world that would pressure us to conform to its own standards instead — a world that might smile indulgently at the "naïve" notions enshrined in the "lovely" words of Jesus as long as they remain non-confrontational and muted in polite and politic society, but that would deem them all along as really a bit silly and "unrealistic." This is a world that will indulge us if we like these pretty sentiments, have them as "inspirational thoughts" on our greeting cards and bookmarks, even worship the one who said them; but otherwise we are not actually supposed to allow them out of the corral to run amok and interfere with "the real world" of politics, business, commerce, taxes, "just" war, and so forth. The moment we abandon really and truly the world's ways and try to live according to Jesus' way, however, and do so visibly and uncompromisingly, we can be sure that we will in time gain notoriety and public contempt and no longer be treated so indulgently. But that means actually living the way as Jesus said to do.

To live as Jesus intended means that we are meant to "drop out" in some ways. That's the challenge I face if I take his words to heart. It means, for example, that I should be apprehensive about donning a uniform if doing so seems to me to be a potential concession to an unjust system or an unjust military. It means I must be skeptical and leery of the importance and fundamental legitimacy of political systems, national claims, patriotism, and legal systems. It means I cannot allow such things to be final arbiters in my worldview. It means I must often be a nonconformist and stay critical of everything demanding my allegiance. It means I must spend time learning to pray and contemplate and cleanse my mind, and that in turn means learning to steer clear of what might distract me from that endeavor or poison my imagination. It means I put Jesus' way first and live life with a certain kind of gracious detachment, sharpened mind, and quiet demeanor. It means learning gentleness, even at the risk of seeming noncommittal or overly passive or just plain stubborn to others. It means that I might be more reclusive or more willing to protest in public or mingle with the down-and-out more fully. Whatever else it means concretely, it means I can't get off the hook once I determine to follow Jesus. Going to church, being religious, even "being a Christian" and adopting a particular set of doctrines about Jesus won't be enough.

The Beatitudes, like the rest of the Sermon on the Mount, introduce a way of life to me. Either I espouse them wholly, or I walk away.

4

The Kingdom of God and the Law of Moses: What Is Meant by "Righteousness"?

—⟨⟩—

5:13 *"You are the salt of the earth; but if salt has lost its taste, how shall its saltness be restored? It is no longer good for anything except to be thrown out and trodden under foot by men.* 14*You are the light of the world. A city set on a hill cannot be hid.* 15*Nor do men light a lamp and put it under a bushel, but on a stand, and it gives light to all in the house.* 16*Let your light so shine before men, that they may see your good works and give glory to your Father who is in heaven.* 17*Think not that I have come to abolish the law and the prophets; I have come not to abolish them but to fulfil them.* 18*For truly, I say to you, till heaven and earth pass away, not an iota, not a dot, will pass from the law until all is accomplished.* 19*Whoever then relaxes one of the least of these commandments and teaches men so, shall be called least in the kingdom of heaven; but he who does them and teaches them shall be called great in the kingdom of heaven.* 20*For I tell you, unless your righteousness exceeds that of the scribes and Pharisees, you will never enter the kingdom of heaven."*

From what follows in the Sermon, it becomes clear that, to understand Jesus' teaching about the kingdom of heaven, the role of the Law of Israel — the Torah (the "Teaching") — is vitally important. What is the nature of the Torah or Law within the kingdom that Jesus proclaims? Not "Torah" merely in the sense of an external inventory of hundreds of commandments, as found in the books of Exodus, Leviticus, Numbers, and Deuteronomy — a list which includes, but is far more exhaustive than, the Ten Commandments (Exod. 20:1-17; Deut. 5:6-21) — but the Torah as it is to be taken inwardly and written on the human heart.

The internalizing of the Law is the very core of the coming "new covenant," as it was characterized in one very important Old Testament prophecy, and which Jesus apparently related to his own mission (cf. Matt. 26:28). It was the prophet Jeremiah (seventh to sixth centuries B.C.), who had announced that there would be a new covenant:

> "Behold, the days are coming, says the LORD, when I will make a new covenant with the house of Israel and the house of Judah, not like the covenant which I made with their fathers when I took them by the hand to bring them out of the land of Egypt, my covenant which they broke, though I was their husband, says the LORD. But this is the covenant which I will make with the house of Israel after those days, says the LORD: I will put my law within them, and I will write it upon their hearts; and I will be their God, and they shall be my people. And no longer shall each man teach his neighbor and each his brother, saying, 'Know the LORD,' for they shall all know me, from the least of them to the greatest, says the LORD; for I will forgive their iniquity, and I will remember their sin no more." (Jer. 31:31-34)

I think that this short passage provides the most foundational subtext for what Jesus means when he speaks of the Torah in reference to the righteousness of the kingdom of heaven. Jeremiah's prophecy declares that not only is there to be a new covenant that will be established in "the days" that "are coming," but that this covenant will *not* be "like the covenant" under Moses. That brings us to ask this question: In just what way will it not be like the former covenant? The answer given by Jeremiah is that it will no longer be rooted in a law taught externally from above, but rooted in a conviction from within. It won't, in other words, be merely *legal.* It won't deal with what lies on the surface of human life, but it will work in a way we moderns would call psychological. It will go beyond and below the "contractual" and regulatory. Instead, it will be a living, interior, motivating reality, one which — once it is made known through Jesus' teaching and our discipleship — will be at work in our conscious and subconscious depths, "written on the heart" by God himself. Those who will enter into this new covenant will thus "know" the Lord, referring to an inner awareness of God. "Knowing," as it is understood in this Hebrew context, is intimate in nature. It is personal and experiential. It is the equivalent of "loving" the Lord in a binding way, as two lovers bind themselves to one another. The promise carries with it an undoubted experiential and mystical dimension.

The Sermon on the Mount, then, turns first and foremost to the observance of the Law, and Jesus — like Jeremiah's prophecy says of the new covenant — will present it as a matter of the heart, that is to say, as a matter of deeply rooted commitment. For the Jewish hearers of Jesus, who placed the Torah at the center of their lives, this focus was critical. For them, the question would inevitably be, What would this radical rabbi say about the Torah? After all, religion for them meant a life lived within a true interpretation of it. It was as fundamental as, say, the Tao is fundamental to Chinese thought or Dharma is to Buddhism. It shaped all of life and established righteousness.

Before all else, then, Jesus taught the Torah afresh, as would have been expected of him by his Jewish hearers. And, quite noticeably, Jesus' elucidation of it would be clearly in accord with the more inward and mystical interpretation already discoverable in the prophets.

"I have not come to abolish the law and the prophets," Jesus therefore reassures us. "I have come not to abolish them but to fulfill them." So, according to his own testimony, he "fulfills" the Torah; he "completes" it. But how? It would seem that he means that the Torah becomes "complete" when it goes into the hearts and lives of his hearers and changes them from the inside out. In other words, when it has a real effect in human hearts and changes human lives, it has been fulfilled: persons become embodiments of the Torah, and the Torah lives in them. This interpretation will be unambiguous in verses 21-48 below, in the series of six "antitheses" that will come later. There Jesus will crack through the shell of the Law's literal statutes, extracting the kernels of their inner meaning, and planting those deep into the motivations and minds of his followers. No longer literal murder, but the anger that prompts it is condemned; no longer simply adultery, but the taproot of lust is dug out; and so forth. In moving the Torah down deep into the inner motivations and passions, Jesus "writes the law upon their hearts." This, then, is the very essence of the new covenant.

"For truly, I say to you, till heaven and earth pass away, not an iota, not a dot, will pass from the law until all is accomplished." Jesus then warns against "relaxing" even "the least of these commandments." We might well ask, "Which commandments?" Does Jesus refer here, for instance, to the dietary laws, or the ritual laws of the Tabernacle, or the laws in Deuteronomy that detail how a king should rule his people? No. None of these matters is even remotely considered by Jesus.

Partly this is due, of course, to the fact that in Jesus' day the ritual laws were in ongoing operation, and would remain so for forty years after his ministry concluded. For the most part, he had no reason to comment on those laws. Still, as the earliest Christians knew for a certainty and the Gospel accounts make evident, he had personally "relaxed" such laws as those regarding the death penalty, the Sabbath regulations, various cleanliness rules, and even the laws related to kosher foods. It seems likely that he would not have insisted that Gentile followers were bound to keep all the laws of the Torah, and there is certainly reason to suppose that he would have taught — just as St. Paul would later teach — that the moral law is something already naturally written within even the hearts of those who don't know the Law of Moses (cf. Rom. 1:13-16). The Torah's moral laws were obviously not a unique or surprising revelation that, say, murder and adultery are wrong — every ancient civilized culture assumed that they were; rather, they showed that what was already known in human nature to be right and wrong was in accord with the nature of God.

So, when it comes to the moral laws of the Torah, we are faced with another characteristic of Jesus' message, one which disturbed even some of his contemporaries. As the Gospels make abundantly clear, his message was inflammatory and roundly denounced by the authorities in Jerusalem. One of the reasons these religious leaders were so incensed by him was his repeatedly (and sometimes pointedly) lax attitude toward the moral laws themselves. He was not strict in their defense, not zealous enough to suit his critics. When it came to a choice between upholding some severe penalty or else preserving a human life, Jesus chose the latter. Whereas the Law commanded the death penalty for a number of infractions, Jesus stood firmly for mercy and forgiveness. In this way his actions frequently defied the literal Law.

In one unforgettable account — unforgettable because early on it was inserted into the Gospel of John, though it had not originally been part of that text, and there it has remained ever since — a woman taken in adultery is allowed to go free, instead of summarily undergoing stoning, because of Jesus' extremely "lax" intervention. He even forgives her (John 7:53–8:11). Jesus is portrayed in this scene as flagrantly defying the clear commandment of the Law of Moses (Lev. 20:10; Deut. 22:23-24).

As already noted, Jesus is not overly concerned with ritual or kosher laws in his teaching. As we shall see, he will touch on Jewish Temple sacrifices, but only as a passing example related to a deeper ethical point. The only aspect of the Law which he addresses directly is the *moral* law, and in this he is most definitely concerned with the "spirit" of the Torah rather than the letter of it. He "spiritualizes" aspects of the Ten Commandments, directing them at the very underpinnings of our minds and wills. He is most concerned with what the Torah means in essence. He is not concerned with legal infringements, rewards and punishments meted out in some sort of "correct" courtroom procedure. He is interested in human lives and how people can live rightly and well.

So he is willing to suspend any literal judgment in the case of palpable sin, such as in the account of the woman's adultery mentioned above, sparing the sinner with almost carefree mercifulness. But he doesn't spare in the least, for instance, the interior vice of lust. Where contaminating inner drives are concerned, he is ruthless. Where people are concerned, he is generous. The Ten Commandments will get a makeover in the Sermon on the Mount, and in the process Jesus will not be "relaxing" the Law at all. When Jesus goes beneath the surface and forces us to examine our secret thoughts and scrutinize the unpleasant drives, passions, inward suggestions, and numerous "unclean spirits" that move us to malevolent behaviors, he is reinforcing the most pure objective of the Law.

Even when he speaks of the threat of "hell" (literally, "Gehenna"), which we will look at below, it isn't in relation to some violation of a mere list of external rules. Rather, it means that the tragic refusal to be inwardly transformed, through the spiritual dynamism of the Torah, can have only the consequence of one's whole life unnecessarily thrown away. This makes sense if we realize that for Jesus, as for all Jews, the Torah was more than a written code. It was a living reality that flowed through all creation from God. Indeed, the Torah was regarded, at least in later Judaism, as older than creation and as being wisdom itself. It's more than likely that Jesus' understanding of it was similar.

So, in effect, not an iota or a dot of the Law — meaning the moral laws — has been compromised by Jesus' radical approach. If the objective of the eternal Torah is accomplished, and lives are transformed and human beings learn to live in wisdom, then nothing contained in the Law — not even its smallest grammatical marks — have been in vain. The Law is fulfilled when people *do* the commandments as if by nature. "In the kingdom of heaven," says Jesus, "he who does them [the commandments] and teaches them shall be called great." In the words of Jeremiah's prophecy, God will put his laws "within them." They will be transformed from within, and thus will *naturally* grow into righteousness. This describes both Jesus' approach to the Torah — how he interprets it — and how he likewise presents the nature of the kingdom of heaven itself. *The kingdom of heaven is to be discovered, therefore, by living in accordance with Jesus' interpretation of the Torah, and nothing else than that.*

Jesus tells a parable, found only in the Gospel of Mark (4:26-29), which suggests this very idea: that the kingdom grows like a living thing within us.

> And he said, "The kingdom of God is as if a man should scatter seed upon the ground, and should sleep and rise night and day, and the seed should sprout and grow, he knows not how. The earth produces of itself, first the blade, then the ear, then the full grain in the ear. But when the grain is ripe, at once he puts in the sickle, because the harvest has come."

Likewise, the Torah as the living seed of the kingdom's righteousness, planted within us through the interpretive teaching of Jesus, becomes more and more at one with our own hearts and minds, our thoughts and actions. This is why Jesus can say to us, "Unless your righteousness exceeds that of the scribes and Pharisees [the guardians of the religious rules and regulations, who preached an outward conformity to all sorts of legal minutiae], you will never enter the kingdom of heaven."

Such living, then, has both its invisible and its visible aspects. Invisibly, like salt giving savor to food, the community of Jesus' disciples is meant to provide, and thus should preserve in itself, its "saltness." If salt isn't salty, says Jesus, it's worthless. "Saltness" is the interior, invisible life lived in relation to God.

Jesus will be talking precisely about this invisible element when he speaks of "secret" prayer and even "secret" almsgiving and fasting. Religious externals are not for parading in public, but for our inner lives, out of sight and not done for the sake of getting kudos from others. Keeping ourselves salty means being authentic, doing what we do invisibly as unto God. That sort of pursuit of God will make us, in a hidden way, all that we should be interiorly.

Without taking care of our selves inwardly, we will have little hope of having anything to give to the world around us. Flight attendants tell us that if we have to put on oxygen masks in a crisis onboard an airplane, we must be sure to put our own on first before trying to assist anybody else. The same principle is true for us in this context: We must first care for our inner lives, and then — from what we gain there — try to be of use to others outside.

Visibly, then, we are to be "the light of the world," out in the open, doing good deeds. These are actions that reveal God's mercy and love, and nothing less. Jesus is emphasizing what we do, how we treat others, how we glorify his Father in the eyes of the world. Deeds speak louder than words. St. Francis of Assisi told his friars to preach the gospel, and sometimes even use words to do it. His directive was, of course, ironic — preaching may be appropriate in certain contexts, but no one longs for lofty and lovely words, but little else.

One of the greatest disservices ever perpetrated by the church was not sufficiently dissuading so many of its own defenders and theologians from declaiming so many things that never really needed to be talked about at all. I forget who said it, but once a teacher of one of the Far Eastern religions made a reference to "poor, talkative Christianity." Sadly, his disparaging remark was all too accurate. No other religion has ever outdone Christianity in producing so many given to speechifying and doctrinal prattle. It isn't as though Jesus had nothing to say about it, either. He plainly warned us against it: "You are not to be called rabbi, for you have one teacher, and you are all brethren" (Matt. 23:8).

What we say must be backed up by what we are. If we are to be authentic interiorly, we are also meant to be that exteriorly as well. A shining light radiates openly — there's no shadow there, nothing concealed. Light is light. So should Jesus' followers be: inwardly true, outwardly true. When people look at his disciples, they are meant to see not the disciples so much as the living fact of God's life lovingly at work in their midst. "Let your light so shine before men, that they may see your good works and give glory" — not to you, but — "to your Father who is in heaven."

THESE, THEN, are the invisible and visible aspects of righteousness, as Jesus presents them to us in metaphors. He will go on, in the "antitheses" that follow, to be more specific about what this righteousness entails, comparing the inner Torah of kingdom life with the mere externalizing of a strictly legal interpretation. What we have seen here is that Jesus' message is, in fact, Torah-centered, but Torah-centered in a generous and transformative way. Legalism is replaced with dynamic life, working from within, and working through our good actions in the world. That, Jesus tells us, is where God will most convincingly be seen by others.

As someone who wishes to be a true disciple of Jesus, this is a message I must take into myself and try to live as sincerely as I can.

5

What Jesus Says about Lust, Anger, and Inconstancy

T he remainder of Matthew 5 is a set of six antitheses between the understanding of the Law as the religious leaders of Jesus' day presented it, and the understanding of it that Jesus imparts. There is much to reflect upon in these verses. In fact, there is so much that I will look at them over the next two chapters. I will explore the first three antitheses here, and the final three antitheses in the next chapter.

As we shall see, Jesus will begin each of these antitheses by saying, "It was said . . . ," followed by a quotation from the Torah familiar to his listeners. He then gives his alternative commandment, which in each case is an intensification of the Law's greater intention, introduced by the words "But I say to you . . ." With each of his radical interpretations of the six laws he brings up, he provides an illustration of its implementation.

The six areas of focus may be said to epitomize the full range of basic ethical concern: the destructive nature of anger, the destructive nature of lust, the need for constancy in the conjugal relationship, the importance of saying simply what we mean and sticking to our word, commitment to nonviolence and non-retaliation, and doing good even to our enemies. Thought, word, and deed are all here. What's more, if these forms of righteousness were practiced universally, the world would not be in the mess it so obviously is. That, of course, is the point.

Jesus is forming a community of those who embrace this righteousness, which is the Torah lived, wisdom embodied, and the kingdom of heaven brought down to earth. It is a community meant to be a visible light of guidance for the world. Again, it can't be stressed enough that Jesus intends that we actually work at living this way.

This is not a program of hopelessness, a standard that cannot be lived. Jesus simply takes for granted that here is a goal well within our power to pursue, certainly with God's help (thus the need for an interior prayer life, as we will explore later), but undoubtedly meant to be received by us as an acceptable objective. There are those Christians who maintain, on dubious doctrinal grounds, that this is an impossible ideal. They say that humanity is "totally depraved" and incapable of any true goodness, so that (in a crude distortion of Isaiah 64:6) "all our righteousness is as filthy rags," and we can't possibly do anything worthwhile in God's eyes without the overriding supernatural power of his grace. What should function as a mitigating factor for these Christians is that there have been numerous non-Christians who have lived their lives as if in keeping with the Sermon on the Mount, whether they knew the text or not. Common sense should tell us that we need to lay aside those features of any theological system that don't take Jesus at his word, or don't make room for the testimony of others' experiences, even if those experiences should happen to those who live outside that system's confessional bounds. Jesus' word in this Sermon is as straightforward as anything of this sort could be. If we want to live it, we will find the grace we need is already there.

What do the six antitheses have to say to us today? Most of them, if not all, should strike resounding chords in us, since we all know what anger, lust, inconstancy, word-breaking, desire for retaliation, and hatred feel like, and how they affect others. These sayings of Jesus will cut into areas we might like to keep untouched and out of sight even from ourselves.

Let's begin by exploring the first three antitheses here.

> *5:21 "You have heard that it was said to the men of old, 'You shall not kill; and whoever kills shall be liable to judgment.' 22But I say to you that every one who is angry with his brother shall be liable to judgment; whoever insults his brother shall be liable to the council, and whoever says, 'You fool!' shall be liable to the hell of fire. 23So if you are offering your gift at the altar, and there remember that your brother has something against you, 24leave your gift there before the altar and go; first be reconciled to your brother, and then come and offer your gift. 25Make friends quickly with your accuser, while you are going with him to court, lest your accuser hand you over to the judge, and the judge to the guard, and you be put in prison; 26truly, I say to you, you will never get out till you have paid the last penny."*

The humanism of Jesus meets us immediately. The vast majority of the teachings of the Sermon on the Mount deal with our relations and actions towards other human beings. The most grievous of all human interactions is the taking of life — murder. Its finality is its most terrible aspect. It cannot be undone, and the perpetrator knows — if he is human enough to feel in his conscience the full weight of what he has done — that no appeasement can ever fully make amends. So it is that Jesus quotes the old law in all its sternness, making it clear that the murderer "is liable to judgment," and not mercy, under its terms (cf. Exod. 20:13; 21:12; Lev. 24:17; Deut. 5:17).

Usually, what motivates an act of murder is some form of anger. It might be a direct and flaring anger against the person killed; or it might be a deeper, simmering, often inchoate anger that produces the sort of psychological monster devoid of either empathy or sympathy, whose violence is not directed toward any particular target. Anyone could be the random victim of the latter. But, whatever form it takes, however its influence works inside one, anger is the culprit and key to murder, and there is something implicitly murderous in it right from the very outset. Anger, then, is Jesus' focus; it is what must be faced and either uprooted or restrained.

Restraint is what Jesus emphasizes. We are not even to insult (literally, "say 'Raca!'" — a term of abuse) or call someone a "fool" (in Greek, *more* — from whence we get the word "moron"). Anger, insult, abuse — these lead to "judgment," "the council" (literally, the "Sanhedrin") of judging elders, and, most horribly, to "hell."

With these images of judgment, Jesus conjures up a Jewish context before our mind's eye. He is describing the community he is building, the fellowship of disciples who seek to live according to the way of the kingdom of heaven. What he is teaching is that the incursions of unrestrained anger should not be tolerated in that context. He does not say that forgiveness isn't possible if an outburst should ever occur. (If such slips were not forgivable, most of us would have reason for dread.) But he is saying that any such action demands immediate redress. He says that, if we are about to approach God with a gift and recall that we have an anger or insult issue to patch up with another, we should drop our religious duty and take care of reconciling with our brother or sister first. Before we go to God with a gift, we go first to "the image of God" who is our neighbor and set things right with that person. Then we may approach God, and only then.

The imagery of the altar and the gift are, of course, related to the Jewish Temple. A second image has to do with the very "council" of judgment to which Jesus alludes earlier. In effect, he is saying that if we have given in to a display of anger or insult or abuse, we still have the opportunity to make amends, and receive mercy from our offended opponent, before we must answer for it. If we refuse to reconcile, then — metaphorically speaking — we will be forced to pay back to the last red cent what we caused in damages. Jesus is using the image of monetary "repayment," but the issue is really about a damaged reputation or a wound inflicted on another by our lack of restraint of anger. It is here that the image of "hell" needs to be mentioned.

Actually, we should avoid the old Norse/Germanic/English word "hell" as unsuitable for what the New Testament depicts under various images, all of them illustrating a "loss" to be avoided at all costs (the word "damnation," derived from the Latin *damnus,* refers to "loss"). The word translated "hell" is, in the original, "Gehenna," and it refers to a valley southwest of Jerusalem that appears to have been used as a garbage dump. Through a long process, the smoldering garbage dump in the Valley of Hinnom (= "Gehenna") became a common symbol for the ultimate loss of one's self, the casting away that followed the final judgment of the value of one's whole life. The "unquenchable fire" and "undying worm" (taken from Isaiah 66:24), found elsewhere to describe the horrors of "Gehenna" (Mark 9:48), were likewise metaphors suggested by the dump — an unpleasant picture of waste and immolation. The warning is implicit to the image: "Do not waste your life. Do not throw your soul away." Other images are in a similar vein. The "outer darkness where there will be weeping and gnashing of teeth" (e.g., Matt. 25:30) is a picture of exclusion, utter loneliness, and abandonment that is unnecessarily brought upon oneself through apathy and willful carelessness, a refusal to receive or hold on to what God freely gives. Again, the warning is implied: "Do not ignore or treat lightly the gifts of God. Do not exclude yourself."

Whatever one is to make, then, of the figurative "Gehenna," it is not a real "place," nor is it a "state of being" (indeed, it suggests, ontologically speaking, the precise opposite). Neither is it an "everlasting place of torment," as if Jesus thought of his heavenly Father as condoning an eternal prison with an eternal torture chamber, the very idea being abhorrent both to the message of Jesus and to common sense.

Neither is it "everlasting" in the texts that mention duration — much less "eternal" — but only (literally) "unto ages of ages." That simply means, in Semitic and Greek usage, "a very long time."

"Gehenna," then, is not to be taken literally. It stands as a symbol for something we wish to avoid, certainly; but what we should want to avoid are not exaggerated concepts of a fairy-tale "hell," like those that have fired prurient and vicious imaginations for far too long. What is to be legitimately feared is the possibility that we can render our lives "no longer good for anything" (see 5:13 above). The image of "Gehenna" is poetic, even if appalling, and it shouldn't be reduced to any of the many metaphors used for an otherwise indescribable condition of self-loss. The idea of a literal "hellfire and damnation" or a literal "eternal torture chamber," beloved of Dominicans and fundamentalists alike, is to misunderstand, add to, and misapply the subtle similes required of poetic language. To collapse the meaning of damnation to the meager dimensions of its metaphors — which are useful enough as suggestive images, but hardly to be taken as descriptive in any literal sense — is to limit ourselves to a few disturbing pictures and a number of logical difficulties.

At any rate, it is anger that brings us to the disturbing realization of how close to the precipice we often stand. Anger, once it seizes our minds, has the power to distort our lives thoroughly. We all have anger within us, of course, and in some cases it is even justified. Jesus himself exhibited anger on more than one occasion. Matthew 23 gives us just one example of a sustained angry denunciation of the scribes and Pharisees on the part of Jesus, and his "cleansing of the temple" in 21:12-16 was an act of righteous outrage.

But the anger that Jesus condemns in this text is of a more insidious kind. It is the sort that lashes out at our neighbors, puts the worst interpretation on others' motives, insists on its own way, is easily annoyed, snappish, insulting, and sometimes cruel. So, says Jesus, get it under control, resist it, tear it out, if you can — but, even if you can't, restrain it. How? Once more, the answer must lie in our inner discipline of prayer and contemplation, a subject that Jesus will address later in the Sermon.

Lastly, a word to my fellow Christians might be appropriate. It may suitably be noted here that there is a sad and shameful fact that we must face — that is, our various churches, under their various ecclesiastical shepherds, have failed to practice reconciliation between one another, have even dared to make such lack of reconciliation part of their official policies and doctrines, have taught their people to obey these artificial rules as if obedience to them amounted to identifying marks of righteousness, and yet — disregarding the words of Jesus — have encouraged their members to approach the altar with their gifts anyway.

There is no more important altar among Jesus' followers than sharing in the communion of Jesus' body and blood, however that action with bread and wine may variously be understood in theory and method. At its most basic, it is a deed that confirms and renews the covenant we have with Jesus and with all his disciples. It is taken from gifts that we bring to the altar, so to speak, and its meaning is one of unity and forgiveness. And yet, notoriously, we still see many churches not permitting their own and others' members to partake of it together, as if the abstract doctrines of each tradition about the concrete action, which Jesus told us to do in memory of him, are more important than what that action itself signifies.

Old rivalries, bitternesses, mutual anathemas, and insults are allowed, even encouraged, to remain and dominate our discipleship, as if we should live under and honor the curses of five hundred, one thousand, or seventeen hundred years ago. So, while denouncing other Christian disciples as heretics or as schismatics or, at the very least, as being in a state of "impaired communion," the churches go forward with their gifts to the altar in a perpetuated state of non-reconciliation. This is a scandal which the world sees, to our shame; but it's one that some of us might just be bold enough to begin to ignore. If members of the clergy want to disbar themselves from each other's communions, that is their sad choice. It needn't be ours. They can wear their regalia and refuse to share the Lord's table. We needn't follow their example, nor be particularly bothered if they urge (or order) us not to go our own way. We shouldn't be angry, insulting, or abusive about it; but we should go right ahead and join one another in Communion whenever the opportunity is there to do so, regardless of institutional prohibitions. The altar belongs to Jesus, and he was clear about our being reconciled with each other. (He was not clear, by comparison, in those thorny doctrinal matters that have historically tended to divide us.) You and I can be reconciled among ourselves, refusing all anger and insults between us, even those of a long-established, conventional, but, in the final analysis, illegitimate nature.

> 5:27 *"You have heard that it was said, 'You shall not commit adultery.'* 28*But I say to you that every one who looks at a woman lustfully has already committed adultery with her in his heart.* 29*If your right eye causes you to sin, pluck it out and throw it away; it is better that you lose one of your members than that your whole body be thrown into hell.* 30*And if your right hand causes you to sin, cut it off and throw it away; it is better that you lose one of your members than that your whole body go into hell."*

Having dealt with anger, Jesus turns our attention to the commandment "You shall not commit adultery." The inducement to adultery is sexual lust.

Before going any further, it is necessary that we distinguish natural sexual desire from what we call "lust." The two are easily confused, especially by those who have been so greatly repressed

WORD OF THE WEEK
The Subject: God ordains certain men to hell on purpose

Isaiah 64:8 - 0 Lord, thou art our Father; we are the clay; and thou our potter; and we all are the work of thy hand.

work - Hebrew: Maaseh · an action (good or bad); product; transaction; business

Romans 9:20-23 - Who art thou that repliest against God? Shall the thing formed say to him that formed it, why hast thou made me thus? Hath not the potter the power over the clay of the same lump, to make one vessel unto honour and another unto dishonour - What if God willing to show his wrath, and to make his power known, endured with much long suffering the vessels of wrath fitted to destruction: And that he might make known the riches of his glory on the vessels of mercy, which he hath afore prepared unto glory.

fitted - Greek: katartizo · to complete thoroughly; fit; frame; arrange; prepare. Thayer says this word speaks of men whose souls God has so constituted that they cannot escape destruction; their mind is fixed that they frame themselves.

Men get angry to think that we serve a God that can do as it pleases him. They actually think that an almighty God thinks the way they think and that he could not possibly form-fit a vessel to hell merely to show his wrath and power. Paul said he does. Men have difficulty perceiving a God that predestinates men (Rom. 8:29) on whom he desires to show his grace (unmerited favor) and mercy, that he may shower them throughout eternity with the riches of his glory. We like to believe that we must give him permission if he is to operate in our hearts and minds. The Lord said, "My thoughts are not your thoughts, neither are your ways my ways. As the heavens are higher than the earth, so are my ways higher than your ways and my thoughts than your thoughts (Isaiah 55:8,9)". Our God is in the heavens: he hath done whatsoever he hath pleased (Psalms 115:3). He doeth whatsoever pleaseth him (Eccl 8:3). Thou, 0 Lord, hast done as it pleased thee (Jonah 1:14). Whatsoever the Lord pleased, that did he in heaven, and earth, and in the seas, and in all deep places (Psalms 135:6). He does all his pleasure (Isa. 46:10; Isa. 44:24-28; Eph. 1:5,9; Philippians 2:13). It is Jesus that holds the keys to death and hell (Rev. 1:18), not Satan. God will intentionally cast these evil vessels of wrath into hell and lock them up for eternity because it is not his pleasure to draw them to him (John 6:44). This doctrine angers men, though it is taught throughout the pages of God's Holy Book. Men do not have a Biblical view of the living God when they think he is not in control of all things including the minds and hearts of all men. God is not only love to the vessels of mercy, but he is a consuming fire (Deut. 4:24) upon the vessels of wrath fitted to destruction. We do not serve a God who is Superman that can only shake mountains, implode blackholes, and explode quasars. The God of the universe can harden and soften the hearts of men at will (Rom. 9:18; Ezek. 36:26). He giveth not account of any of his matters (Job 33:13).

GRACE AND TRUTH MINISTRIES
P.O. Box 1109, Hendersonville, TN 37077
Jim Brown - Bible Teacher · Local: (615) 824-8502 | Toll Free: (800) 625-5409
https://www.graceandtruth.net/

in sexual matters — often the result of strict religious upbringing — that they have come to regard all sexual feelings, especially their own, as inherently sinful and dirty. Of course, when sex, already considered unclean and something forbidden, and thus fascinating and attractive in consequence, is then mixed with the easily accessible pornography of today, obsession with it can become almost a mania — and, with many persons, it definitely is just that.

Healthy sexual feelings are those that can take pleasure in the thought of sex itself, can admire the beauty of the human body, include thankfulness for the gift of sexual intimacy and the bodily union with the one who is loved, are casual and relaxed about the subject. Sexual desire is a cause neither for fear nor for excessive fascination. It is part of life. It has a tang and an excitement about it that is particularly pleasing and worth cherishing within the covenanted friendship of marriage, and it precludes guilt. A healthy attitude towards sex is also realistic enough to recognize that aging will lessen sexual desire over time (despite Viagra and other sexual stimulants people think they need for the sake of their happiness), and that old age is a time for garnering wisdom and preparing for the great journey of death. A healthy sexual attitude is mature, at ease, humorous.

Lust, on the other hand, is the opposite of love. Love gives; lust takes. Love gazes at the other as another person. Lust doesn't rightly see another person; it sees instead an object existing for its own gratification. It objectifies that which should be another subject. "Thou" becomes "it." If lust does see another person at all, it sees that person as something to possess, dominate, and pollute. Lust sometimes is mixed up with anger, hatred, and resentment, and it has a violent streak in it — especially with men who have chips on their shoulders regarding women — that is ugly, defiling, and sub-human. Pornography in our culture has made it seem that there is virtually no image too explicit and no sexual deviancy too repellent that it can't be indulged in the imagination.

Nothing is taboo or unthinkable, and — thanks to the Internet — it can all be found for free. Any child can look it up online. It's doubtful that healthy sexual feelings can develop in such a context without the sort of discipline and oversight that too few care to exercise.

Jesus plainly nails sexual lust as an evil passion within us that should not be stimulated or pampered. His warning is sharp and severe: "If your right eye causes you to sin [literally, 'to stumble'], pluck it out and throw it away; it is better that you lose one of your members than that your whole body be thrown into hell ['Gehenna' = the garbage dump, as commented upon above]. And if your right hand causes you to sin ['stumble'], cut it off and throw it away; it is better that you lose one of your members than that your whole body go into hell ['Gehenna']." The language here is, of course, not to be taken literally. Again, Jesus speaks in metaphors and uses poetic imagery. Jewish rabbis used hyperbole — useful exaggeration and overstatement — to emphasize particularly important points. If something needed to be stressed — and the danger of lust certainly needs to be stressed — then strong and unforgettable language was used.

Jesus means that the right eye and the right hand (considered in ancient times to be of greater worth than the left eye and the left hand) should not look at or touch whatever is defiling. In modern terms, we should, for example, stay clear of pornographic images. If it means that we put a locking system designed for families on our computers so that certain Web sites can't be easily accessed, then so be it. If it means that we use our computers only where others are present and can spot whatever we're looking at, if it means that we steer clear of certain parts of town, avoid particular places in a bookstore, and so on, then we do these things. The point is not that we maim ourselves, but that we "pluck out" and "cut off" those temptations that arouse our otherwise embryonic lust. We don't want to give it the least chance of growing in us.

The word for "woman" used in the Greek text ("every one who looks at a woman") is *gyne* — and refers, therefore, to a married woman. In light of this rather fine point of biblical exegesis, two things might beneficially be mentioned.

First, this fact doesn't give a man license to look at an *unmarried* woman with lust. The issue is not the status of the woman in question, but the nature of the lust that motivates unhealthy sexual imagination and action. Here Jesus is primarily concerned to preserve the covenantal integrity of a marriage. No man has the right to look at another man's wife lustfully; and within the Palestinian society of Jesus' day, every woman was either married or had in the works an arrangement, through her family, to be married. Betrothal, for example, was regarded just as binding as marriage itself. So, Jesus was saying that marriage is not to be invaded by another's lust, and lust itself is to be amputated from the heart.

Within marriage, of course, sexual desire is to be satisfying and enjoyed. Jesus was, after all, Jewish — not a Greco-Roman ascetic in background. His own celibacy had to do with prophetic calling (not uncommon, even among Jews), not with any distaste for normal sexual relations or the goodness of marriage.

Second, although Jesus refers to men lusting after women, and not the other way around, it should be taken for granted that lust can be a problem for women, too. To the extent that it is a disruptive presence in a woman's life, it should meet with the same spiritual resistance that is expected of men.

Again, it is lust, not healthy sexual desire, that needs to be denied. For some persons, learning the difference between the two may well prove to be a very great challenge. In our age, this is sadly more difficult than it was in earlier times. The power of the media image is largely to blame for this, and we may all need to find ways to reduce our "image intake" — fasting from media, taking retreats, going out more into natural surroundings, becoming re-acquainted with books in place of television, and so on.

5:31"It was also said, 'Whoever divorces his wife, let him give her a certificate of divorce.' 32But I say to you that every one who divorces his wife, except on the ground of unchastity, makes her an adulteress; and whoever marries a divorced woman commits adultery."

Deuteronomy 24:1-4 is the background for this antithesis, and the theme follows closely upon that of the preceding passage. It is also a passage that has a parallel passage later in Matthew (19:3-9), in which Jesus replies to a question posed to him by Pharisees: "Is it lawful for one to divorce one's wife for any cause?" There Jesus responds at greater length than he does in the short antithesis we have here. There he says:

> "Have you not read that he who made them from the beginning made them male and female, and said, 'For this reason a man shall leave his father and mother and be joined to his wife, and the two shall become one flesh'? So they are no longer two but one flesh. What therefore God has joined together, let not man put asunder." They said to him, "Why then did Moses command one to give a certificate of divorce, and to put her away?" He said to them, "For your hardness of heart Moses allowed you to divorce your wives, but from the beginning it was not so. And I say to you: whoever divorces his wife, except for unchastity, and marries another, commits adultery."

This passage is immediately followed by a commendation (not a mandate for anyone, including the "ordained") of the celibate life as a way to serve God prophetically with whole-heartedness (19:10-12). And this is followed by the blessing of children (19:13-15). In other words, all states of life in discipleship — marriage, celibacy, and childhood — receive Jesus' full blessing and support.

If we look more closely at those three states, we might notice a barely visible common thread. That culture did not regard children as important persons in their own right. Jesus, in contradistinction, held children up as exemplars of true discipleship (teachableness and openness): "Let the children come to me, and do not hinder them; for to such belongs the kingdom of heaven" (19:14).

As for celibates, they certainly were not absent in Jewish culture in Jesus' day. The Essenes, for example, valued committed celibacy, and the prophets had often been celibates. Afire with the Spirit of God, prophets were wholly in his service (e.g., Elijah and Elisha, Jeremiah, Daniel, and, of course, John the Baptist). But, even given that fact, there was also the notion among the more common folk that the unmarried man was only "half a man"; and Jesus' comparison of the dedicated celibate with the despised category of the eunuch ("there are eunuchs who have made themselves eunuchs for the sake of the kingdom of heaven" — 19:12) suggests that pursuing such a calling must have elicited some amount of scorn from others. To call a man a "eunuch" was not any more a compliment then than it would be today. Jesus disregards such derision and uses the term boldly, in defiance of social tastes. More than that, under the Law of Moses, a eunuch was not allowed to "enter the assembly of the LORD" (Deut. 23:1). Jesus' use of the term was thus deeply provocative.

The common theme, then, is this: Who is disrespected in society, but instead should be recognized in the kingdom of heaven as intrinsically of value? Jesus' answer to this implied question in these passages is children, "eunuchs," and, unquestionably, *women* as well.

It is a remarkable fact that Jesus treated women as equals — remarkable because in that culture, women, like children and celibates, were not supposed to be accorded such dignity. But Jesus put up no barriers with women. He enjoyed their company and hospitality. He loved them as friends. They sat before him as disciples and traveled with the men who followed him. They subsidized his itinerant ministry (cf. Luke 8:1-3). They were the first witnesses of his resurrection — in a day when a woman's testimony in a court case was inadmissible simply because of her sex. In this place and time, Jesus' constant regard for women was unheard of among his peers. He broke down the barriers with an ease that is understated in the Gospels, but that we know to have been unusual and very likely shocking to his contemporaries. So it is that Jesus upholds the marriage bond as inviolable in these texts.

Returning to our antithesis in the Sermon on the Mount, then, it is quite right that, following what Jesus had to say about the nature of lust from outside a marriage, we hear about the threat to a woman's care and safety from within a marriage. The issue is the integrity of the marriage covenant, in which women in that society were protected from poverty and all the ills that go with it. If a marriage dissolved in ancient Palestine, it would be due to a man's decision within a marriage, and possibly the consequence of a man's intrusion into another man's marriage. Jesus had condemned lusting after a *gyne,* as noted above, which means first and foremost a *married woman,* another man's wife. This prohibition warned a man from *outside* not to destroy another man's marriage (and "unchastity" or "immorality" — *porneia* — is, as Jesus allows, considered a legitimate cause for divorce). Now, with this antithesis, he turns his attention to the husband *within* a marriage.

Only men could procure divorces, and so Jesus naturally targets the men. Women had no such prerogative. If a man grew tired of his older, less alluring, less pleasing wife, he could dismiss her and arrange to take up with a more pleasing alternative, perhaps the ex-wife of another. Jesus says no to all this. From outside a given marriage, he says, men are not to lust after other men's wives. From within any given marriage, he goes on, husbands are not to dismiss their wives ("for any cause," in the words of the Pharisees; but only "on the ground of unchastity," as Jesus says here — in other words, if there has been some complicity between the wife and another man in an immoral act).

Remarriage was sometimes a possibility for "dismissed" women. But Jesus' prohibition was meant to protect women from the more usual circumstances with which divorce left them: having no means to live and no place to go, needing to beg in the streets to survive, and very possibly becoming prostitutes to support themselves. (If you have ever wondered where all those prostitutes came from in the "pious" Jewish society of Jesus' day, here is the chief cause of it.) From the beginning, Jesus says in the Matthew 19 passage, men (and women) were intended to live within their covenant commitment as if they were "one flesh." Constancy is to be practiced. Inconstancy, just like lust, is to be avoided.

Thus, a man's remarrying simply to cast aside one wife for another could be tantamount to active "adultery" on his part ("whoever marries a divorced woman commits adultery"); at the same time, he could be guilty of abandoning his former wife to the potentially humiliating condition of (in the passive tense) *moicheuthenai* — literally, a situation of being seduced adulterously ("every one who divorces his wife, except on the ground of unchastity, makes her an adulteress"). It is not at all unlikely that this passive condition of adulterous seduction refers to a state of prostitution, just as much as to any possible remarriage. In effect, such a society tacitly allows for wife-swapping, serial monogamy, and prostitution — hardly a society in which women would be very highly valued.

What does this say to us today in a society in which marriage is arranged differently (for example, couples choose one another; their families don't choose their partners for them), in which women have equal right to divorce their husbands, and in which divorce usually doesn't have the same drastic consequences for women as it did in Jesus' day? It seems that, despite the very great differences, the basic principle of marriage as covenant remains. It should be maintained with integrity, and kept from threats that might come from both within and without.

Further, and more seriously, there are the issues with which Jesus does not engage. As I have admitted, I am a divorced and remarried man myself; how should I respond to the tough strictures that Jesus enunciates in both Matthew 5 and Matthew 19? There are marriages that end because of abuse, physical and/or psycho-logical in nature. There are, as we know, marriages that are unsafe for one of the spouses and/or any children involved. There are, in fact, persons who marry and should never have done so; or who have married without any real understanding of what they were doing or the commitment that was expected of them. Marriages fall apart for numerous reasons, and Jesus doesn't deal with these. To be absolutely clear, he deals with the institution of his day and with the questions of his day. In Jesus' day the issue of "grounds" for divorce was a passionate one — one in which two rabbinical perspectives were even at odds. When those Pharisees asked his opinion on the matter in Matthew 19, they were throwing him a hot potato. Jesus' own strictness on the subject, as I've noted, had to do with the consequences of divorce in that society — conse-quences that often made women *victims.*

There are *marriages,* however, in which both women and men can be the victims. In such cases, divorce may in reality prove to be the rescue most needed for the parties involved, although it should always be a last resort in a situation proven to be impossi-ble. And, if I dare to say it, a good remarriage may be a source of healing. If Jesus' concern is really with those who find themselves in positions of victimization, threat, abuse, psychological flatten-ing, and so on, then we must allow for the possibility — as most Christian bodies have in one form or another — that there can be reasons for the dissolution of a failed or misunderstood covenant, and even reasons for a new and better one.

Divorce is never something to celebrate (even if a healthy re-marriage might prove to be), and often people are hurt and rela-tionships are strained in even the most justifiable divorce. To ad-mit that there can be just causes for some divorces in no way changes the essential teaching of Jesus here. Neither lust nor in-constancy is a small matter. Both are seeds for disaster and mis-ery. Both are to be denied and avoided strenuously.

6

What Jesus Says about Word-Breaking, Retaliation, and Hatred

———✦✦✦———

> *5:33 "Again you have heard that it was said to the men of old, 'You shall not swear falsely, but shall perform to the Lord what you have sworn.' 34But I say to you, Do not swear at all, either by heaven, for it is the throne of God, 35or by the earth, for it is his footstool, or by Jerusalem, for it is the city of the great King. 36And do not swear by your head, for you cannot make one hair white or black. 37Let what you say be simply 'Yes' or 'No'; anything more than this comes from evil."*

The Law permitted making vows to the Lord (Lev. 19:12; Num. 30:2; Deut. 23:21). Jesus, on the other hand, says that we should not make vows at all, but rather say only what we will or will not do before God. We should not swear by heaven, earth, the holy city of Jerusalem, or even by our own heads. In poetic terms, he tells us that none of these — even our own heads! — belongs to us: heaven is God's throne, the earth his footstool, Jerusalem the city of the great King (referring either to God or, possibly, to the dynasty of David), and we don't even have a say about the true color of our own hair. "Let what you say be simply 'Yes' or 'No'; anything more than this comes from evil [or 'the Evil One']." In case we miss it, this is very tough language. Swearing oaths is not only not recommended, it is downright wrong to do. "Evil" is a very strong word to use to describe it.

That the early Christians took this injunction quite seriously is seen in how the Epistle of James virtually repeats Jesus' saying — indeed, stressing it (note the first three words, which I italicize): "*But above all,* my brethren, do not swear, either by heaven or by earth or with any other oath, but let your yes be yes and your no be no, that you may not fall under condemnation" (James 5:12).

It would seem that Jesus' (and James's) meaning is not to over-reach one's own human limitations, two of which are implied. First, why should we *vow* to do anything, placing ourselves under such a burden that — given unforeseen circumstances — we might prove unable to carry through to the end? Why should we put ourselves in a position of ever possibly breaking an oath? To do so may, in effect, be a capitulation to the Evil One's desire to humiliate and accuse us (which was precisely how the devil was understood in Jesus' culture — a tempter and trickster who delighted in causing those striving to be righteous to fail, and then rubbing their noses in it). In that sense, it could prove evil and potentially condemning for those who, while seeking to do right, become ensnared instead through their own boasting.

And boasting is what an oath actually is — and that's the second human limitation. As Jesus suggests, there is nothing over which we have so much say or control that we can make an oath in its name — not even the hair of our own heads. We are here today, gone tomorrow. It is best if we learn to be men and women of few words, limit ourselves to "yes" and "no," and still be prepared for the possibility that we may not be able to fulfill all we wish to accomplish, or avoid all we wish to avoid. Our own power is imperfect; we are flesh and blood and frail. We ought to be persons of integrity, standing on our own two feet, keeping our words as best we can, and not given to making inflated vows, whether religious or civil. Paradoxically, it is in our humility that we stand strong and true. The less rhetoric, the more authentic.

In a world that would seek to put us under binding obligations of all sorts — civic, military, political, financial, ecclesiastical, what have you — it is best that we pick and choose just what our commitments should be. Where obligations, commitments, and membership in anything are concerned, less is more. "Yes" or "No" is quite sufficient; and of the two, "No" probably should be the more frequently said.

> 5:38 *"You have heard that it was said, 'An eye for an eye and a tooth for a tooth.' 39But I say to you, Do not resist one who is evil. But if any one strikes you on the right cheek, turn to him the other also; 40and if any one would sue you and take your coat, let him have your cloak as well; 41and if any one forces you to go one mile, go with him two miles. 42Give to him who begs from you, and do not refuse him who would borrow from you."*

The fifth antithesis is moving us in the direction of the sixth and climactic antithesis. The "law of retaliation" (the Latin term *lex talionis* is often found in commentaries and theology books to designate this), which is found in three places in the Torah, is quoted by Jesus (cf. Exod. 21:22-25; Lev. 24:19-21; Deut. 19:16-21). Originally, this was a *restriction* on vengeance. One could receive satisfaction for damages suffered *only* to the extent of the damages themselves. In other words, if one was injured by another in some way, the injured party couldn't exact revenge by killing the offender. A commensurate recompense was all that could be exacted. Nothing more. Justice meant proportionality — "eye for eye, tooth for tooth, life for life," not "a life for a tooth."

Jesus drastically alters this accepted understanding of justice. Justice, he says, is not only *not* exacting more than is proportionate for a harm done; it is positively not exacting recompense or revenge at all ("Do not resist one who is evil" — i.e., one "who does bad to you"). Indeed, it may mean responding to an injustice not in kind, but in generosity. He gives four examples of injustice, and four ways to respond.

If someone strikes you on your right cheek, Jesus says, turn to him the other. That means, in fact, a defiant act. If someone shames you, stand your ground, but don't resort to the moral level of the person who has shamed you. It is important to note that the "other" cheek is the left cheek. The left side was associated with "dishonor," and the right with honor. To turn the left side toward one who strikes you is bold and resistant, but nonviolent. It shows lack of respect, an unyielding stance, but also a refusal to hit back. It turns the shaming back upon the would-be shamer. As is well-known, in the last century Gandhi in India and Martin Luther King Jr. in the United States, along with those they inspired in their respective contexts, understood well and exemplified this form of non-retaliation. They did so in the name of justice, and they were willing to suffer the personal consequences aimed at them for the sake of a greater cause. Both derived their ethic of nonviolent resistance from the teachings of Jesus.

Jesus continues with a second example: If someone sues you in court and demands one of your garments for settlement, give it to him, and add another if you have one. The issue here is a legal one, and — it would seem in the context — an abusive use of the legal process by someone unscrupulous enough even to take the clothes off another's back. Jesus says that such a one should be humbled by giving to him even more than he demands in a court of law. Jesus utterly turns the *lex talionis* on its head here. As we will soon see, this is in complete agreement with his attitude toward property in general.

As sometimes happened, a Roman soldier would grab a Palestinian and force him to carry his gear or to do his labor for him. We may recall, for instance, how Roman soldiers "compelled" Simon of Cyrene to carry Jesus' cross on the way to his crucifixion (Matt.

27:32). Jesus says, Go along with the bully. In fact, humble him by going twice the distance he demands of you. Offer kindness and diligence. (It might alter his attitude; but even if it doesn't, you have risen above the situation and the moral level of the bully.) You may get nothing in return but a sore back and sore feet, but you may have given the oppressor some food for thought to chew on. The goal is, as Paul the Apostle put it, not to "be overcome by evil, but [to] overcome evil with good" (Rom. 12:21).

As for beggars and borrowers, Jesus says that we should be openhanded. I would add that this is a good policy, even if we think we're being conned by the person begging. In fact, in this particular context, Jesus seems to imply that, if we suspect that we are dealing with a dishonest beggar or a "borrower" who is somewhat less than reliable in the matter of returning what he has borrowed, we should nonetheless not refuse to give or lend. As Jesus will go on to say about almsgiving: "Do not let your left hand know what your right hand is doing." Again, we are beginning to see how Jesus would have us care for and make use of our property. The appropriate word for it is not "carelessness" or "negligence," but "detachment." And "detachment" means that we can detach our selves from it, and it from our selves. A significant point here is that, just as we should not hesitate to give more to one who demands of us unjustly, neither should we demand from the beggar or borrower what we have turned over to them, even if it might prove to be "just" to do so. Jesus, by the way, makes no distinction between the "deserving" and the "undeserving" poor. Detachment means not noticing or judging according to such "qualifications" when in the act of generosity.

The terms of "justice" for Jesus are not equality and fairness. Jesus apparently doesn't care if it's "fair" or not, whether it's "equal" or "proportionate" or not. He is for non-retaliation, no exaction of recompense, no taking of revenge, and for openhanded generosity and detachment. They want it? Give it, and give even more. They took it? Let them keep it. You gave it or lent it? Don't bother to demand it back. (I would be tempted to add "unless it's a book, of course" — but, then, I'd just be interpolating with my own culpable weakness.)

This, then, sets us up for the decisive and fundamental antithesis that follows.

> ⁵:⁴³ "You have heard that it was said, 'You shall love your neighbor and hate your enemy.' ⁴⁴But I say to you, Love your enemies and pray for those who persecute you, ⁴⁵so that you may be sons of your Father who is in heaven; for he makes his sun rise on the evil and on the good, and sends rain on the just and on the unjust. ⁴⁶For if you love those who love you, what reward have you? Do not even the tax collectors do the same? ⁴⁷And if you salute only your brethren, what more are you doing than others? Do not even the Gentiles do the same? ⁴⁸You, therefore, must be perfect, as your heavenly Father is perfect."

We may notice that Jesus' quotation right at the outset is not taken directly from the Torah. In Leviticus 19:18, we read, "You shall not take vengeance or bear any grudge against the sons of your own people, but you shall love your neighbor as yourself: I am the LORD."

If we think it stops there, with "the sons of your own people," we are mistaken; for the Law goes on to teach that even Gentiles living among the Hebrew people are to be treated well: "When a stranger sojourns with you in your land, you shall not do him wrong. The stranger who sojourns with you shall be to you as the native among you, and you shall love him as yourself; for you were strangers in the land of Egypt: I am the LORD" (Lev. 19:33-34). So, according to the Law, even the stranger — the Gentile — is to be loved as oneself, and not treated with disrespect or cruelty. So, where does the idea of "hating your enemy," which Jesus quotes, come from?

It was apparently an interpretation added to the commandment that had become popular by the time of Jesus, possibly in reaction to the treatment of the Jews historically by their Gentile overlords. We see such a sentiment expressed in the Dead Sea Scrolls, for example, where it is enjoined that "the Children of Light" are to hate "the Children of Darkness" (1QS 1:9-10). But, of course, we see the same sentiment expressed much earlier, and in canonical scripture itself. A particularly notorious example is that of Psalm 137:8-9, in which the psalmist gives voice to Judah's cry for vengeance upon her rapacious Babylonian subjugators: "O daughter of Babylon, you devastator! Happy shall he be who requites you with what you have done to us! Happy shall he be who takes your little ones and dashes them against the rock!" Given the horror of the atrocities perpetrated by Babylon on Judah, as we know from the recorded histories of the event, it is little wonder that such an outcry for justice should have been a result.

But there are other voices in the Bible which teach a different message. To give one example, there is the four-chapter parable we call the book of Jonah. It is a very late book in the Old Testament, certainly unhistorical, filled with what C. S. Lewis called good "Jewish humor" and rich in Hebrew puns, but with a very serious message. The point of the whole short story is that, whereas the prophet Jonah is angry and bitter at the enemies of Israel, God is merciful. The Assyrians had been as cruel in their conquering of the northern kingdom of Israel as Babylonians would be to the Southern kingdom of Judah at a later date. The Assyrian Ninevites would have been regarded by the readers of Jonah with much the same sort of loathing as twentieth-century and twenty-first-century Jews might regard the Nazis. Jonah clearly wants to see God destroy them, "nuke" them, if you will, off the face of the earth. But God doesn't agree with Jonah's desire for revenge. At the crucial moment, Nineveh repents — changes its mind and heart and pleads for mercy — and God forgives. Although God had threatened them with destruction, he now shows himself to be merciful. The "punch line" of the book, which is addressed to a fuming Jonah in the story, is actually being addressed to its Jewish readers, whose attitude toward the Gentiles was often one of anxiety and dislike: "And should not I pity Nineveh, that great city, in which there are more than a hundred and twenty thousand persons who do not know their right hand from their left [children?], and also much cattle?" (Jonah 4:11). The book concludes with that barbed question, and every reader is meant to ask whether he or she sides with Jonah and his anger, hating the "other," or with God and his universal mercy.

Jesus asks the same question of us, in essence. Do we think that to love our neighbors allows us — or even requires us — to hate our enemies? The answer is an unequivocal no. We are not simply to be satisfied with loving only those who love us, or greeting only those who greet us. (For Jews, this meant voicing the blessing to the one who had greeted them with "Shalom," which means "Peace.") To be so limited is no better than to be like tax collectors, who worked in collusion with the Gentiles, or like the Gentiles themselves. (If this sort of comment offends some of us non-Jews, we must bear in mind that Jesus was a Jew and spoke like a rabbi to his fellow Jews.) We are to love and wish peace to all persons — and Jesus meant that this peace should be extended to us Gentiles as well.

This brings up an important question: What does Jesus mean by "love"? And, a little further on in the passage, what does he mean when he exhorts us to be "perfect"? These two words, seemingly so simple and succinct, are also terribly misunderstood and misapplied all too frequently.

The first thing to mention is that these two words go together in the passage. In other words, when Jesus speaks of "perfection," he is saying something about our "love." The word for "perfect" in Greek is *teleios,* and it refers to making something "complete," or bringing something to the "end" and "goal" for which it exists and toward which it tends. It likewise means "maturity." When Jesus says, "You, therefore, must be perfect, as your heavenly Father is perfect," he is referring to the subject of the passage, which is "love." The disciple must be as "perfect" in love — that is, as "complete" or as fully loving of all — as God himself is.

It is interesting that Luke renders this teaching of Jesus in a more direct way, and it is worth quoting the full parallel passage as we find it there (Luke 6:32-36):

> "If you love those who love you, what credit is that to you? For even sinners love those who love them. And if you do good to those who do good to you, what credit is that to you? For even sinners do the same. And if you lend to those from whom you hope to receive, what credit is that to you? Even sinners lend to sinners, to receive as much again. But love your enemies, and do good, and lend, expecting nothing in return; and your reward will be great, and you will be sons of the Most High; for he is kind to the ungrateful and the selfish. Be merciful, even as your Father is merciful."

Unlike Matthew, who refers to tax collectors and Gentiles, Luke speaks of "sinners," which literally means those who stray from the right course. More to the point, he speaks of "doing good" and "lending" to others. Like Matthew, Luke points out that God is kind to all, even to the undeserving: "He is kind to the ungrateful and the selfish." Matthew reveals God as working behind the impersonal forces of nature: "For he makes his sun rise on the evil and on the good, and sends rain on the just and the unjust." Someone might counter that nature also throws up some rather terrible things as well — tsunamis, earthquakes, tornadoes, hurricanes, forest fires, famines, predation, etcetera, etcetera. By implication, should God be held accountable for these as well? It is a fair question, but one which Jesus does not deal with here. In this instance, he is referring only to the recurring seasons, the planting and harvest, and how the natural world cooperates with the efforts of human beings, regardless of their moral uprightness or lack thereof. Finally, instead of echoing Matthew's exhortation to "perfection," Luke changes the terminology entirely: "Be merciful, even as your Father is merciful."

This is the place to bring in one more important aspect of what Jesus means when he refers to "the kingdom of God." It can be construed that he drew on such descriptions of it as found, for example, in Psalm 145. Verses 8-16 of that text portray it this way:

> The LORD is gracious and **merciful**,
> slow to anger and abounding in steadfast **love**.
> The LORD is good to **all**,
> and his compassion is over **all** that he has made.
> All thy works shall give thanks to thee, O LORD,
> and all thy saints shall bless thee!
> They shall speak of the glory of thy **kingdom**,
> and tell of thy power,
> to make known to the sons of men thy mighty deeds,
> and the glorious splendor of thy **kingdom**.
> **Thy kingdom is an everlasting kingdom**,
> and thy dominion endures throughout all generations.
> The LORD is faithful in all his words,
> and gracious in all his deeds.
> The LORD upholds all who are falling,
> and raises up all who are bowed down.
> **The eyes of all look to thee,**
> **and thou givest them their food in due season.**
> **Thou openest thy hand,**
> **thou satisfiest the desire of every living thing.**

I have put some of the significant words and lines in bold type merely to highlight the connection with Jesus' teachings. A moment's reflection on these verses reveals that God's kingdom is revealed, as in Jesus' description of it, precisely by his compassion, mercy, and love for all — distributed impartially and through the natural order of planting and reaping. His kingdom is both transcendent ("everlasting") and immanent, as seen in his provision of food to every living — and hungry — thing. Impartial loving deeds, then, characterize God and his kingdom. It is the very essence of all that the word "righteousness" means in the Sermon on the Mount, that quality and disposition which Jesus' disciples are to have in greater measure than that seen in the desiccated religion of the scribes and Pharisees (Matt. 5:20). Jesus' disciples, then, are to mirror the revealed character of God, and thus "make known to the sons of men" through their own actions God's "mighty deeds" (Matt. 5:16).

Returning to the word "love," we can now begin to see that in neither Matthew nor Luke does it refer to one's *feelings* of love, but — as Luke clarifies it — it is synonymous with *doing good.* The Greek word *agapate* — from *agape* — means "benefaction." It is not a word of feeling or sentiment so much as a word of action — it refers to "support" and "aid" of another, of "caring." The objection that most people have to Jesus' exhortation to love all — as also the objection many have to "forgiveness" — is often based on the false idea that Jesus is saying that one must *feel love* for all. And, of course, that is impossible for us to do. But we can be prepared *to do good* to all who cross our path or come within the sphere of our influence, *regardless of how we might feel about them.* Indeed, the point of the passage, and its parallel in Luke, is precisely that we should work against our prejudices, anger, dislikes, hatreds, and maybe even our desires for revenge, and do good anyway. "Love" is "doing good," pure and simple, and doing it to all — "the evil and the good," "the just and the unjust," or, in Luke's terms, "sinners." Frankly, we can do it. We just *choose* not to do so time and time again. Jesus tells us to change our behavior. He says nothing about our feelings.

Love is practical and active. That's the vital point here — it is the goal we should set for ourselves. We should be as "complete" in this respect as God, who works within and through the impersonal forces, the ebb and flow, of nature. Nature simply does what it does; the sun rises and the rain falls, heedless of whom it benefits. Graciousness and kindness should be serene and impartial. Feelings of hatred, personal dislikes, bigotry, and other ways we have of justifying our lack of generosity toward select persons should all be ignored as unfit for disciples of Jesus. Whatever our resentments, feelings of antagonism, or almost instinctual reactions of aversion toward anyone or any group, we are called to rise above our feelings and simply do good to them. In doing so, we practice love.

Looking back over the six antitheses, we can consider anger, lust, divorce, the making and breaking of vows, and the desire for retaliation from the perspective of this final and crowning teaching on love. If we love/do good, we will guard ourselves against anger, and hold our tongues to keep from insulting and verbally abusing others. If we love/do good, we will seek to see others as persons, not as objects for our own depersonalizing gratification. If we love/do good, we will seek to maintain our marriage covenant. If we love/do good, we will not make foolish vows or break our word; and we will speak succinctly and truly. If we love/do good, we will resist our own wishes for avenging insult and injury done against us. Ultimately, we seek to be perfect — complete — in love and the generous doing of good.

Paul, the great interpreter of Jesus to the Gentiles, recognized this aspect of Jesus' teaching about love: that it was the crucial factor in living the Torah, and thereby living in the kingdom of God. He put the matter this way:

> Owe no one anything, except to love one another; for he who loves his neighbor has fulfilled the law. The commandments, "You shall not commit adultery, You shall not kill, You shall not steal, You shall not covet," and any other commandment, are summed up in this sentence, "You shall love your neighbor as

yourself." Love does no wrong to a neighbor; therefore love is the fulfilling of the law. (Rom. 13:8-10)

There it is in a nutshell: *Love of neighbor is the fulfilling of the Law of God.* It is the message of the kingdom, as we have seen, reduced to its purest essence.

Jesus has applied the Law to the deepest layers of our selves. This is where the seed of the kingdom of God is planted: within us, in our "hearts," the center of our being. Here we must begin to be living Torahs, from the inside out. So now Jesus turns our attention to the great Jewish practices of almsgiving, prayer, and fasting. In our piety, or spirituality, we can find the inner resources to live according to the definitive interpretation of the Law that Jesus gives us.

7

Our Secret Lives of Righteousness

———✒———

G od works secretly, in a hidden fashion, behind the scenes,
when he causes his sun to rise and his rain to fall. Behind the
movements of creation are the secret actions of a divine dynamism. God is invisible, beyond our grasp, except through the
grace we see operative in nature. We could call this the normal
righteousness of God — his continuous "right action" toward all
things. Growth, change, life's countless adaptations and forms,
the mysteries of space and time, all these and everything we can
possibly know or experience "live, move, and have their being" in
God (see Acts 17:28), and yet he is beyond our direct knowing.

There is a sense, to use anthropomorphic language, in which
we can speak of the humility of God. Despite those moments in
the Bible when he is described as speaking in fire and thunder,
there is the more profound revelation that he is better perceived
in "a still small voice" (1 Kings 19:12): "Be still and know that I am
God" (Ps. 46:10). Jesus, we are told, often slipped off alone to
pray, unseen by his disciples. He would go to be still and know
his Father's presence, listening for the still small voice. Perhaps
it was especially in those moments that he would also observe
the ways of birds, take notice of the flowers, and watch the farm-

ing and other activities of his fellow villagers — images he would employ in his sayings and parables. These he might observe and contemplate, possibly, while he communed with God; and he might see in these humble things analogies of the work of God himself. The work of God is what we would also understand by God's "righteousness." "Righteousness" (in Greek, *dikaiosune*) in Jewish thought means, above all, *deeds* of justice — good and right *doings*.

The word translated as "piety" in Matthew 6:1 is also *dikaiosune* — "righteousness." The implication is that our righteousness is to be a response to, and an echo of, God's righteousness. Jesus has already warned us in the Sermon on the Mount that "unless your righteousness exceeds that of the scribes and Pharisees, you will never enter the kingdom of heaven" (5:20). Having completed his radicalizing of the Torah in his six antitheses, then, he now turns to our righteousness, our deeds, or — as our translation renders it — our "piety." As God's righteousness is subtle and secret, so, we find, should ours be.

> 6:1 *"Beware of practicing your piety before men in order to be seen by them; for then you will have no reward from your Father who is in heaven."*

The first word, "Beware," is a strong one. We are to be especially careful not to parade our works in public, seeking admiration in a sensational manner.

At first blush, this may appear to contradict Jesus' earlier statement that we are to be "the light of the world" and a "city set on a hill," which is to say, in plain view, with our good works visible to the world so that our Father may be glorified. But there is no real contradiction between the earlier imperative to be openly visible and this one to be quietly reticent.

The "good works" Jesus refers to in the earlier passage are charitable acts that cannot help but be seen. There he means such things as caring for the needs of the poor and sick in practical ways. Here, though, he refers to three recognizably "religious" devotional practices (almsgiving, prayer, and fasting) — works that would be seen to be "pious" and "devout" publicly, that would draw attention to the external signs of our religious behavior. He warns us that making big public gestures of piety are to be guarded against. Precisely what should be avoided are those outward things and actions that show others just how religious we are. The more we put our religiousness on display, the more potential we have to be ashamed. Jesus wants his followers to be known not for their religious displays but for their loving deeds.

The warning is against hypocrisy. We are not to be, as Jesus will say repeatedly, like the "hypocrites." The word "hypocrites" is a neutral term, meaning stage actors. In the ancient world, actors wore masks when they performed onstage. Jesus is saying that doing public religious actions in order to impress onlookers is like play-acting with masks on. The true face remains hidden; all that is seen is the production, the play. But behind the mask of respectability might be any disposition; and Jesus is interested in the quality of our dispositions, not in our public performances of religiosity.

In fact, to be very honest, when we think of religion, we often think first of its external and public aspects — the costumes, the drama, the liturgies or services, the elevation of individuals in the congregation who give more than others or who pray more conspicuously, or clergy who preach with outstanding fervor and eloquence. In and of themselves, these may be fine things; but they do not constitute the real nature of righteousness, and righteousness is the true business of religion. And it is with the true business of religion that we are to be occupied. True religion is inward, hidden, and dispositional; it is a matter of character. Character in turn is seen in action.

As with the Law in the previous passages, piety will be radicalized by Jesus — that is, taken down to its unseen *roots*. In other words, piety is to be seen as a matter of the heart, an aspect primarily of our secret lives, and not ostentatious.

In Judaism, almsgiving, prayer, and fasting were all considered essential to the life of the pious Jew. A practitioner of the Torah would practice all three as evidence of his covenantal faith. Jesus no more abolishes these practices than he does the Law and the Prophets. But he does insist that they be inward disciplines before all else.

8

The Practice of Almsgiving

—⟨∞⟩—

Jesus begins his discussion of essential practices with the practice of almsgiving, perhaps the most "outward" of the deeds of righteousness:

> *6:2 "Thus, when you give alms, sound no trumpet before you, as the hypocrites do in the synagogues and in the streets, that they may be praised by men. Truly, I say to you, they have received their reward. 3But when you give alms, do not let your left hand know what your right hand is doing, 4so that your alms may be in secret; and your Father who sees in secret will reward you."*

Was there a practice of "sounding the trumpet" in the synagogue and streets when there was to be a public distribution of alms? Did the local synagogue do this to make a public — indeed, liturgical — display of its generosity? It seems that this was the case. It certainly may have drawn the poor to the place of donation, where they would have been met by their public benefactors.

Two things come of this sort of public exhibition. First, the donators come off looking good to the general observers, and such recognition has its perks (as every baby-kissing, glad-handing politician running for office knows). Second, however, the poor are forced to come out into the open if they want to receive something, and their need is also made a spectacle. If the rich and respectable have the chance to show off their liberality, the poor get their "chance" to show off their poverty. It is bad enough to be impoverished, but this is surely an additional humiliation, and all so the well-off may "be praised by men." (In the United States today, for instance, with its morality of money making the man, the one thing that is really regarded as unforgivable and shameful is to be poor. You can steal or lie or murder your spouse and get away with it, and even be admired for it, but to be poor is to be treated in our society as the ultimate moral failure.)

Regarding those parading their almsgiving in public, Jesus has this ironic comment, which he will repeat again when he speaks about prayer and fasting: "They have received their reward." In other words, the applause from the crowd will be the only reward they will ever get. Nothing from God, nothing of immortal worth — just their "fifteen minutes of fame."

Jesus turns to us. When we give to the poor, as we are expected to do, we should avoid glorifying ourselves and humiliating them. Even if we can't manage to give anonymously, anonymous giving is still to be preferred above any demonstration before others. "Do not let your left hand know what your right hand is doing," says Jesus, "so that your alms may be in secret [or 'the secret place']; and your Father who sees in secret [or 'the secret place'] will reward you." Almsgiving is to be "in secret" or, possibly, "within the secret place." Where is this secret place? I believe Jesus means what is often called "the heart." When a giver keeps his or her alms "secret," Jesus is saying, only "the heart" — the core of the giver's conscience, feelings, and thoughts — knows what has been done. It is an exchange that protects the giver from egotism and the receiver from humiliation. The right hand has provided the gift, but the left hand is kept in the dark. This is a metaphor with a touch of the mystical about it. It means that, in some way, we hide the deed even from ourselves. We don't dwell on it, congratulate ourselves over it, but instead move on to other things. In effect, it reminds us of another saying of Jesus recorded in Luke's Gospel: "When you have done all that is commanded you, say, 'We are unworthy servants; we have only done what was our duty'" (Luke 17:10).

God, says Jesus, will reward us. The word for "reward" means "to restore"; in other words, what we give will come back to us in some way. We will have lost nothing by being generous. There is a flow of goods in the kingdom of heaven — or there should be. This idea lies behind Jesus' saying "Every one who has left houses or brothers or sisters or father or mother or children or lands, for my name's sake, will receive a hundredfold, and inherit eternal life" (Matt. 19:29). Ideally, the community of Jesus' disciples is to be a family with shared goods.

Equality among members is supposed to be a value, and in the early days of Christianity it was. We have, for example, the witness of the book of Acts: "All who believed were together and had all things in common; and they sold their possessions and goods and distributed them to all, as any had need" (Acts 2:44-45). The apostle Paul understood this equality as involving whole communities extending their financial aid to other Christian communities when there was urgent reason for it. So it is that he writes to the Christians in the Greek city of Corinth, asking them to aid the poor disciples in Jerusalem who are going through a rough period: "As a matter of equality your abundance at the present time should supply their want, so that their abundance may supply your want, that there may be equality" (2 Cor. 8:14). This was a principle among the early disciples of Jesus. Almsgiving was a means of sharing, establishing equality, and distributing to those in need. This was meant to be reciprocal, and all were called upon — even the poor — to contribute to the common good. In this way, the dignity of all was meant to be upheld, and no one person's ego was allowed to rise above the equality shared by all. Every gift was expected to be appreciated, every member loved, but none unduly revered or indulged. No one community or church was intended to dominate another, but all were to help other Christian communities stay afloat in goods and finances.

It is still an ideal we could aim for, and question — indeed, doubt — those voices that would tell us that this early Christian model of almsgiving, equality, distribution, and dignity could never be realized in today's church or world. Such voices exist, and they can sound very plausible to us. They are sober voices, solemn voices, and they talk a lot about realism in economics, just as those who espouse *realpolitik* tell those opposing war that they are naïve. Nonetheless, we should be suspicious of those who tell us that Jesus' way is not doable, especially if they call themselves Christians. What underlies such cynicism? The big question really is, What do they fear to lose? Don't they realize that Jesus had a lot to say about finances, and none of it had to do with financial security or the accumulation of personal wealth?

At any rate, if we are disciples, we need to think of ways we can put Jesus' authentic ideals into practice.

9

The Practice of Prayer

——◦◦◦◦——

6:5 "And when you pray, you must not be like the hypocrites; for they love to stand and pray in the synagogues and at the street corners, that they may be seen by men. Truly, I say to you, they have received their reward. 6But when you pray, go into your room and shut the door and pray to your Father who is in secret; and your Father who sees in secret will reward you. 7And in praying do not heap up empty phrases as the Gentiles do; for they think that they will be heard for their many words. 8Do not be like them, for your Father knows what you need before you ask him. 9Pray then like this: Our Father who art in heaven, hallowed be thy name. 10Thy kingdom come. Thy will be done, on earth as it is in heaven. 11Give us this day our daily bread. 12And forgive us our debts, as we also have forgiven our debtors. 13And lead us not into temptation, but deliver us from evil. 14For if you forgive men their trespasses, your heavenly Father also will forgive you; 15but if you do not forgive men their trespasses, neither will your Father forgive your trespasses."

When we turn to the subject of prayer, we are dealing with what is most naturally considered "interior" or "secret," a matter of "the heart." Yet, we know that prayer can become a production and play-acting, a matter of the lips alone. Jesus is shown delivering a harsh denunciation of the Pharisees on this very point: "You hypocrites [actors]! Well did Isaiah prophesy of you when he said: 'This people honors me with their lips, but their heart is far from me'" (Matt. 15:7-8; cf. Isa. 29:13). This was not merely a problem for the Pharisees of Jesus' day. We do well to read his reproof of them as a couched warning to his own disciples.

Very possibly we have witnessed elaborate rituals with lengthy liturgical prayers, as if God requires these things to be appeased; or we have witnessed those persons of the long-winded variety who seem to think God has poor hearing or distracted thinking, so that only verbosity and volume can get them a hearing on high. Speaking only for myself, I love magnificent liturgy. My background and inclination make me favor the all-stops-out glory of high-church Anglicanism. But, there and in other traditions, caution is needed. Because our lips have said and sung good things in a public setting, and now our hearts feel "strangely warmed," it is all too easy to believe that in fact our hearts must be close to God. Jesus would have us bring our hearts close to God first "in secret," quietly and not sensationally, and keep them there, whether we are in public or in private.

This demands a discipline for each of us individually. "When you pray, go into your room," says Jesus, "and shut the door and pray to your Father who is in secret [or 'the secret place']; and your Father who sees in secret [or 'the secret place'] will reward you." "You" in this verse is in the singular, not the plural. Jesus is speaking here to us as individuals. Each one of us is meant to develop a secret, hidden, private practice of communion with God. We are to go into our "room" and "shut the door." This is not something intended to be taken literally. It is a metaphor. The "inner room" is Jesus' meaning — that is to say, the inner person or "the heart." It is the secret place in which we encounter the Father for ourselves: he is *our Father,* too; not only the Father of Jesus, but shared with us by Jesus. To know this relationship for ourselves, we must make the effort to get to know him.

One term for this inner dimension of prayer has classically been "mysticism," which makes it sound a whole lot spookier than it is. Other terms are "contemplation" and "meditation," terms that have rather artificially been differentiated.

"Mysticism," in the most basic sense, simply means something "hidden" or "secret." It could be said, without any embarrassment about it, that mysticism is what we most need in our lives to be truly healthy and sane, but it usually comes up against resistance in one way or another. Sometimes we resist it within ourselves. And, of course, our noisy world is a place that does its level best to keep us ever agitated, ever purchasing its "stuff," and ever indebted to it. The societies we live in today demand our time, drain our energy, and want our money. Between bureaucratic red tape, crushing financial worries, and the drugging effects of a ubiquitous entertainment industry which keeps us pacified if not at peace, there is little room left for anything deeper. If there's anything we positively need to be saved from, it's from our culture before it kills our spirits.

The reason that the mystical dimension in our lives is so resisted, both by inside and by outside forces, is simple enough: silence, meditation, contemplation, wonder, being "in secret" and alone with God — these things are fundamentally subversive. None of us likes subversion, being by nature conservative when it comes to our own lives, our immediate survival, and our desire for security. We don't readily take to change, or uncertainty, or insecurity, or to too much open-endedness. And we instinctively and correctly know that contemplative practice, despite its outer stillness and inner peace, will in time have unforeseeable effects in our lives. There need not be any socially manipulative conspiracy against it; we are likely to resist it ourselves unless we are determined and courageous enough to practice solitude, attentiveness, and silence regularly.

Mysticism tends to overthrow whole worlds, both within our selves and outside us. It uproots the status quo, overturns the moneychangers' tables, rearranges our mental furniture, disturbs our complacency, alters our consciousness, and forces us to be true to ourselves and to all things just when we were feeling that being false felt just fine. It disrupts us to the foundations, to the roots of our mental and emotional mountains, when we take contemplative practice seriously.

However, if we are willing to practice contemplation *habitually,* going step by step, we will over time (and it will take time and constant practice) lose the fear of insecurity, and come to a secure point of operating out of a center deep within our selves. We will find we can dispense with getting our sense of security and safety and certainty from outside, and discover it instead flowing from within as from an interior reservoir. More and more we will come to view the world with a freer, calmer, and more confident mind — one that knows, for example, that government leaders can't manipulate us any longer with ideologies and incitements to sham patriotism; that worldly bureaucracies may bully us sometimes, but that they can't really undermine our ability to think or live independently of them; and that occasional overweening religious officials have no real power to distance us from God despite imperious claims to be his indispensable brokers.

Contemplation has the effect of grounding us in something more enduring and real than this transitory existence. It doesn't lull us into a state of stupor, oblivious and dreamy. It isn't looking for "the ultimate trip" or "special graces" or romantic interludes with the heavenly Bridegroom. It isn't after the sensational "locution" here, or the sublimated sensuality of a "vision" there. It isn't "mysticism" in the sickly sweet and "misty" sense of popular depictions we may have seen, nor is it a search for "private revelation." Those who seek such things, or confuse them with mysticism, trivialize God and the limitless magnitude of being. If contemplation is the real thing, though, it wakes us up. We see all things in God, and we see the needs of earth and humanity with sharper clarity. The one thing in all the world that isn't an "opiate of the masses" is religion in its truest, most mystical form. Whatever dope our culture or society might be trying to sell us this week, it is mysticism that keeps us clean and sober.

There is another reason that the mystical dimension is resisted. Contemplation is not entertaining, and we have taught ourselves — or allowed ourselves to be propagandized into believing — that unless we are entertained by or at least preoccupied with something, we will almost immediately become bored. We unconsciously dread boredom because it throws us back upon our inner resources, and we're often unaware that we have any. Actually, we all need to be bored sometimes just to develop some genuine inner resources — just to be creative and imaginative and fully human. Boredom, it can be argued, has had a vital role to play in the history of civilization. Practicing contemplation will involve stretches of silence that are simply dry and dull. Teachers of the spiritual life have always seen such times as beneficial, motivating us to develop habits that go beyond the realm of seeking good feelings. Dry times force us to look for God beyond "god" — that is, to go deeper than our ideas about God, our concepts and images. If we get stuck on any concept, we have a potential idol on our hands, because the mystery of God is infinite in meaning and scope. Boredom tests our resolve to stay serious and sober-minded. If we stick with the practice, boredom will in time dissipate. We will gain something better than experiencing occasional good feelings — we will learn contentment and serenity.

Properly understood, too, "mysticism" has to do with "mystery"; and "mystery" refers to that which cannot be delineated or demarcated, which is illimitable, even if the real presence of mystery has made itself known to our minds. In other words, we intuit the reality of mystery in the sense of awe and wonder.

We can "think" about whatever is mysterious only as we think about any experience of beauty and grandeur; we can think about it in much the same way we can "think" about infinity or self-denying love or the nature of nature: in other words, we can *imagine* it or write *poetically* about it. But then we must be silent about it. Too much description and too many definitions only dispel it.

The "way of the heart" is a term that has often been used for Christian mysticism in its purest sense, and it's a good one. The heart is, as anatomists can confirm, a "thinking organ." Neurologically speaking, it is directly connected to the brain, and so we can say that it has always been an appropriate symbol for the very center of our consciousness. In the mystical practice of the Christian East, contemplative discipline has long been referred to as "the bringing of the mind into the heart" and accompanied with a bodily posture conducive to this end — a deliberate focus on one's core. Another, less widely known phrase, speaks of "imprisoning" one's mind in prayer and keeping it there. This may sound rather negative to our modern ears, but the idea is much the same as going to one's center and abiding there, blocking out other thoughts and intentions for a time. Speaking of the *heart* as a "way" of the disciple's *mind* is to use an ancient metaphor that is ever valid.

This does not involve reflection on rational theology, a mistake often made by earnest Christians, but something quite like the antithesis of that. In its earliest traditional usage, the word "theology" itself referred to prayer, and most pointedly to *contemplative* prayer. It was engagement with the mystery we cannot describe — what the Christian tradition means when it speaks of "apophatic" theology (meaning that which cannot be said except through denial — in other words, that which can be best understood in terms only of "*not* this and *not* that"), or, in Latin, "the negative path" *(via negativa).* Everything that can be said positively about God (i.e., in the language of Western rational theology, that he is being itself, self-existent, above and beyond all things, necessary, one, infinitely perfect, simple in essence, unchanging, great, eternal, the principle of thought, etc.) must be countered by saying that none of these attributes can actually be conceived because God transcends all such categories of human thought and rational expression.

I don't want to deny the place of reason — to do so would be unreasonable. But I do want to qualify rational categories with the frank admission that they are insufficient. To "reason" about God authentically is to know right from the outset two things: that such reasoning is related to what surpasses it without end; and that the language used is analogical at best and of less value to us than the silence of contemplation. So, whatever God is, he isn't "love" as we think of love on a human level; he isn't "almighty" as we think of it in terms of human might; he isn't "being" as we know being, precisely because he is "uncreated being" — and that is far beyond our ability even to begin to comprehend; he isn't any number of adjectives we are accustomed to say he is. Yet, he is present in every aspect of existence — "in him we live and move and have our being"; or, in the words of the grand old Welsh hymn of W. C. Smith, "To all life thou givest, to both great and small;/*In all life thou livest, the true life of all;*/We blossom and flourish, like leaves on the tree,/Then wither and perish; but naught changeth thee."

God is transcendent of all creation, joined inextricably to the creation, simultaneously known and unknowable. He is the mystery within, beside, and above all things, dwelling beyond the ineffable and closer to us than our own souls. Sometimes, in our contemplation, we are very nearly pantheists (God *is* everything), panentheists (God is *in* everything), and transcendentalists (God is *beyond* everything) all at once — and does it matter? No, it emphatically doesn't matter in the least. Prayer is experiential, and God can be trusted to guide our thinking about our experiences later. He is beyond all our categories of thought; and our prayer should not immediately be preoccupied with sorting out the "correct" concepts. We should just get on with prayer itself. Concepts can obscure; but contemplation goes through the curtain — at least it goes far enough so that we can perceive that there *is* a curtain and also a reality on the other side just beyond our sight.

Bringing the mind into the heart, then, has a dimension that we might call philosophical in nature. It is *theological,* too, in the sense I mentioned above, that "theology" originally meant the action of prayer and contemplation. But, philosophically, it is like those philosophies of the Far East, which seek to silence the mind and that chattering little monkey ego of ours during the time of meditation. It is to refuse to conceptualize or depend on rational categories while we are "in secret" with God. It is to allow reality to be simply what it is, as it breaks over us, as God *is* immediately to our consciousness, without stopping to gauge whether or not the experience fits neatly into this or that categorical preconception.

For this to happen, we must search out such things that engender or trigger wonder within us, that awaken awe and the sense of presence in and around all things. Needless to say, the more our minds are dulled by the glitz and glamour, the sensational and shallow, and the diseased and deadening aspects of our contemporary culture in our non-contemplative hours, the less wonder and peace we can hope to enjoy in our contemplative moments.

To exist is to dwell in mystery; to live is — all by itself — a miracle of incalculable worth. To see, to hear, to touch, to taste, to inhale and smell this earth, to come from nothing and pass into infinity, to possess consciousness and the awareness of consciousness (a human quality), to be able to love, to feel, to grieve, to laugh, to know sorrow, to know joy, to praise and feel gratitude to God for the reality in which we are privileged to participate — *to be human* — is to begin to pray. It is, in fact, to be both potentially and actually a mystic and a contemplative. As we are able, with our mind in our hearts, we dwell in stillness with God, even while living in a world of insane activities; and there we find the free and stable center where nothing — not man or the devil — can ever overthrow us. "God is our refuge and strength" (Ps. 46:1a).

Turning our attention to the vocal prayer Jesus teaches us — what has come to be known as the Lord's Prayer or the "Our Father" — we see how intentionally simple and spare it is. It is the opposite of "heaped-up, empty phrases," in other words, the elaborate formulas and incantations used in the Gentiles' rituals and "mystery religions." It is meant to be the fundamental prayer, a simple "yes" being "yes" and "no" being "no," straightforward and unadorned in its plainness. Before contemplative silence, there are just these unfussy phrases and minimal petitions. It is not meant to be the "supreme" prayer, but rather the "basic" one.

Everything hinges on the word "Father" — God understood in his role as "head of the house" and "provider." All of his creation, as Matthew 5:45 reminded us, and which 6:26-30 will go on to suggest, is his household. The word for house in Greek — *oikos* — is the stem from which such words as "economy," "ecumenical," and "ecology" derive. God is the great economist, ecumenist, and ecologist, since he provides all we need to live and thrive in unity with one another. A "father" was, in Jesus' world, a "householder." So, to pray to "our Father" is to pray to the one who gives and sustains.

If Jesus has exhorted us to practice private prayer, he now reminds us that we are praying privately within a fellowship of other, privately praying individuals. God is *our* Father, not merely *my* Father. The prayer I pray, then, in my heart to God, I pray on behalf of all. I "hallow" his name, which means I honor him as "holy" and sacred. He is above all that is, "the one in whom I live, move, and have my being." I pray that his kingdom — the kingdom of *heaven* — come, which is exactly the same thing as "thy will be done on earth as it is [done] in heaven." It is not merely a prayer that it should come in the future, but that it might come *now*. Indeed, I'm praying that it come *into me* right now, and that his will be done on earth, here and now, through me and the other followers of Jesus' way.

88

Fulton County Library System

Customer Name:
 BURNETT, DAKARAI ANANDO (MR)
Customer ID: ******7091

Items that you checked out

Title: Taking Jesus at his word : what Jesus
        really said in the Sermon on the mount
ID: R0120103251
Due: 3/17/2022 11:59 PM

Total items: 1
Account balance: $0.00
2/17/2022 3:16 PM
Checked out: 1
Overdue: 0
Hold requests: 0
Ready for pickup: 0

www.afpls.org

I pray next for our food, today's and tomorrow's, that we would have those essential things we depend upon for physical life. This is not, as medieval commentators sometimes said, a prayer for the sacrament. It is a simple prayer for sustenance.

It is followed by another, very basic prayer, one that likely has real economics in mind. "Forgive us our debts, as we also have forgiven our debtors" means, most likely, just what it says. May what we owe (God?) be pardoned to the extent that we freely release our own debtors of their obligation to pay us back (recall 5:42 and 6:3!).

As was the case in most of the civilized ages but our own, pardoning debts was regarded as an act of virtue and righteousness. Jesus underscores this here. It is possible that this refers to forgiving sins (see below), as it appears in Luke's shorter version of the prayer. However, it is interesting to note how Luke renders it: "And forgive us our sins [*hamartias* = 'strayings'], for we ourselves forgive every one who *is indebted* [*opheilonti*] to us" (Luke 11:4, emphasis mine). In Luke it appears that our willingness to forgive others' *debts* to us invites God's forgiveness of our *sins*. Our acts of lifting the material burden off the shoulders of those who owe us some kind of payback in turn invites God's lifting of spiritual burdens from our conscience.

That such concern for the material welfare of others wins a spiritual reward is something that early Christians accepted as true to the nature of God. It is seen, for instance, in the passages about Cornelius, the Gentile centurion, whose prayers and contributions to the poor won for him a deeper knowledge of Jesus and his kingdom: "About the ninth hour of the day [three P.M.] he saw clearly in a vision an angel ['messenger'] of God coming in and saying to him, 'Cornelius . . . Your prayers and your alms *have ascended as a memorial before God*'" (Acts 10:3-4, emphasis mine; see also 10:30-33). Cornelius is then told to call for Peter, who will tell him about the way of Jesus. Pardoning others their debts to us and giving freely to those in need invite the favor and forgiveness of God for ourselves. Generosity is, to be sure, a sign of repentance on our part — a sign that we are allowing our minds to be changed by the teaching of Jesus.

The prayer concludes with a plea for protection: for rescue when we're tempted to stray from the ways of God, and for deliverance from evil, or — more literally — "the Evil One." The reference is to the devil here. The Hebrew concept of him is as "the adversary" who accuses us. The devil in this cultural setting was more a "devil's advocate" than the devil we often see depicted in art and literature, the horned beast of later lurid imagination. The devil's job (if I might put it that way) was to trip us up, and then accuse us for our trespasses against God. Jesus' prayer is that we may be delivered from his aggravations and bullying. If we stumble and fall, may we get up and start again — not lie there or give up, or let guilt drive us to distress or despair.

So, Jesus' prayer is actually more humane in this final clause, as throughout the entire prayer, than "apocalyptic" or concerned with "supernatural" matters. It has to do with practical matters of discouragement in the face of temptation and, possibly, persecution.

Lastly, Jesus speaks of forgiveness: "For if you forgive men their trespasses [literally, 'lapses'], your heavenly Father also will forgive you; but if you do not forgive men their trespasses ['lapses'], neither will your Father forgive your trespasses ['lapses']."

Prayer deepens one's sense of peace, but peace is also beneficial for deepening one's prayer. Inner peace and true prayer are reciprocal. To get and hold on to peace within oneself, one needs to seek peace outside oneself. The theme in these verses takes us back to 5:23-26 above: Before we approach God, we need to be right with our brothers and sisters, and also with anyone else with whom we have strained relations. Realistically, this may not always prove possible, but we should seek to forgive those who have hurt or angered us, and in the process establish peace within ourselves.

The term rendered "trespasses" here is better translated as

"lapses," and it is not the same word used in verse 12 (a word that is accurately translated there as "debts"). "Lapses" are the things we should have done but failed to do. The word's root refers to "falling away," and in this case it means "falling away" from, or "falling short" of, doing the right thing. Jesus assumes that we have such lapses — "fallings away" or "failings" — in relation to God. We should have done thus and so, but we didn't, or we did something else entirely. The teaching of Jesus also suggests that the Father wishes to forgive — or overlook and let go of — such lapses on our part. He has no need or desire to keep a record of wrongs. Neither, then, says Jesus, should we keep a record of others' wrongs. If we are "children" of this "Father," then we should try to be like him.

Again, let us recall what Jesus says we see the Father doing: "He makes his sun rise on the evil and the good, and sends rain on the just and on the unjust. . . . You, therefore, must be perfect [in your love], as your heavenly Father is [in his]" (5:45, 48). In biblical thinking, forgiveness, like love, is not a feeling but an action. It is a mark of impartiality, and of refusing to allow our feelings or passions to bully us into straying from the way of righteousness. It is one aspect of doing good, and it means — quite simply — "to let go" of something. In this case, it means to let go of any intention of retaliation, of getting even, or of getting back what one thinks one is owed by another. It is letting go of anger, not letting it dominate one's heart and behavior. Even if one has sustained grave hurt from another, even abuse or injury to one's self or someone else whom one loves, the right thing to do is seek to let go of seeking vengeance.

Justice may be required, but not mere blind vengeance. Even if the matter, whatever it may be, must be dealt with in a court of law because it involves a crime of violence, one must desire only that justice is done for the sake of others who could potentially be harmed by the same perpetrator. The desire that the perpetrator should suffer or die or restore something as a punishment, or else *we* will not be satisfied — such a desire is to let in something that will eat at one's insides like a cancer. Bitterness, resentment, and anger must be countered by a refusal to act upon them. Even if such emotions do not dissipate, and possibly *never* dissipate entirely, one can still find a measure of peace by letting go and walking away from attempting any act of revenge. We are not to seek satisfaction for ourselves. If we are honest, we know we will never feel satisfied anyway. Nothing we do to get satisfaction will give us anything but greater hardness of heart, misery, and bitterness. The anger will certainly never go away through such means, and the frustration of knowing that our vengeance accomplished nothing will remain. Jesus says that the way out is to give it up. Just give it up.

Forgiveness, therefore, may be an attempt to mend fences or build bridges, to make some sort of overture to another to restore a strained or broken relationship. Sometimes, maybe often, that will work beautifully. But, just as often perhaps, it may not include any such attempt. The best way to love one's "enemies" in some specific instances may, in fact, be to leave them alone entirely, get distance from them, and simply do no harm to them either by word or deed. Forgiveness of a psychological or physical abuser may precisely be to escape further harm at his or her hands and tongue. One can pray for such a person from a safe distance, and over time the pain and resentment may subside somewhat or — sometimes — subside completely. But, if one avoids doing direct harm (even though litigation may still be advisable in some exceptional circumstances) one has "let go" — one has "forgiven" another.

Forgiveness, like love, is practicable. It is realistic, not dreamy or emotional. It has less to do with one's feelings than with one's determination to let go of past hurts. Peace may come back slowly within. Meditation can help us with that, teaching us to be quiet, focused, and open to God's peace, and we will need to be earnest, consistent, and patient in practicing it. We will need to spend time regularly "in secret" with our Father.

One can liken forgiveness to the Chinese idea of *wu wei* — "non-action" or "actionless action." What that means is knowing when and when *not* to act in a given situation. Sometimes "non-action" is the right action. Sometimes, too, forgiveness is best achieved through our non-action. It is, in fact, *not acting* against someone, even when one feels justly motivated to do so. It is practicing non-retaliation and non-harm. *It is love expressed by letting go and not doing.*

If one can practice forgiveness in this way, one can find peace for prayer. The way of Jesus links prayer and prayer's effectiveness in our lives with our willingness to let go of doing harm toward all others.

10

The Practice of Fasting

—⟨∽∘∽⟩—

6:16 "And when you fast, do not look dismal, like the hypocrites, for they disfigure their faces that their fasting may be seen by men. Truly, I say to you, they have received their reward. 17But when you fast, anoint your head and wash your face, 18that your fasting may not be seen by men but by your Father who is in secret; and your Father who sees in secret will reward you."

In Jewish practice, fasting and prayer went very much together. Jews fasted twice weekly, a custom picked up by early Christians. The traditional days for fasting, from the apostolic age onward, were Wednesday (the day on which Jesus was said to have been betrayed) and Friday (the day of his crucifixion). Jesus here gives no specific weekdays for fasting, but he assumes that his disciples will continue the practice. Fasting was thought to give greater intensity to prayer. In the spirit of the influential passage in the book of Isaiah, fasting was related as well to the needs of the poor and to almsgiving:

> Behold, you fast only to quarrel and to fight and to hit with wicked fist. Fasting like yours this day will not make your voice

to be heard on high. Is such the fast that I choose, a day for a man to humble himself? Is it to bow down his head like a rush, and to spread sackcloth and ashes under him? Will you call this a fast, and a day acceptable to the LORD? Is not this the fast that I choose: to loose the bonds of wickedness, to undo the thongs of the yoke, to let the oppressed go free, and to break every yoke? Is it not to share your bread with the hungry, and bring the homeless poor into your house; when you see the naked, to cover him, and not to hide yourself from your own flesh? Then shall your light break forth like the dawn, and your healing shall spring up speedily; your righteousness shall go before you, the glory of the LORD shall be your rear guard. Then you shall call, and the LORD will answer; you shall cry, and he will say, Here I am. If you take away from the midst of you the yoke, the pointing of the finger, and speaking wickedness, if you pour yourself out for the hungry and satisfy the desire of the afflicted, then shall your light rise in the darkness and your gloom be as the noonday. (Isa. 58:4-10)

With this passage, composed some six centuries before, we can glimpse the mind of Jesus as well. Just as Jesus condemned mere liturgy and religious posturing among the religious leaders of his day, Isaiah condemns those same things here. It was expected practice on special days of fasting to look drawn and haggard, to pull out the sackcloth and ashes, and to make a display out of the whole thing. The prophet points out the incongruity between the outward religious show on such holy days and the sort of quarreling and violence engaged in by the same persons the other days of the year. Instead, says the prophet, what God desires is righteous action in caring for the needy, the homeless, the hungry, and the oppressed. Real fasting is not just giving up food, and it certainly isn't about showing off one's best sackcloth wardrobe and fashionably ashen face; true fasting involves correcting injustice and acting compassionately. If you deal with those latter things, God will come to you.

There isn't much difference here between that age and its religiosity and, say, the sight of a wealthy cutthroat of a Catholic or Episcopalian businessman who attends church on Ash Wednesday, gets his forehead marked with the traditional cross of ashes, noticeably fasts from meat and dessert, and goes about the rest of the day sporting the ashes on his face as a sign of his devotion. His business practices may be vicious most of the year, just barely honest, savagely capitalistic, and injurious to the less advantaged near and far, but his devotion on Ash Wednesday is heartfelt and even a touch sentimental. It makes him feel good; he gets to demonstrate his faith. Perhaps he's a member of Opus Dei and attends St. Patrick's Cathedral, or perhaps he's a member of the Vestry of St. Thomas, Fifth Avenue. Perhaps he gave a fat check for the new pipe organ recently, and the organ has a big brass plaque with his name engraved on it. He's renowned as a benefactor. The message of Isaiah to this man, and Jesus' message as well, would be that none of this can be called true religion at all. True religion would be the transformation of the man himself, and that would be visible in how he conducted his business in the future. The story of Scrooge rests entirely on Jesus' teachings, and those of Isaiah as well. The sign of the reality of this man's religion would not be his religious activities but the practical details of his workday living. The other things — church attendance, the Ash Wednesday service, the brass plaque on the organ — may all have their place, and perhaps they might even suggest something worthy about the man. But how he lives and works, and not his expressions of piety, are what really and lastingly matter for the disciple of Jesus.

Jesus tells us that fasting — like almsgiving and prayer — is not something to be paraded. We are to keep our faces washed, and especially of those ashes after an Ash Wednesday service, and to put away the sackcloth. No one is supposed to know how "religious" we are. Real fasting means we give from what we have and learn to curb our appetites. Real fasting may mean eating less expensive food, not going to the swankest restaurants, and not being a practical narcissist. It may mean not buying the most elaborate cell phone on the market, the biggest car, the best entertainment system — maybe going without some of these altogether. Real fasting, especially in our consumerist culture, means to stand apart from the unthinking point of view that we are what we buy. We may need to reduce our time given over to entertainment and self-gratification in order to have time for others' needs.

Fasting is not strictly a matter of food and drink. It has to do with how we eat, certainly; but also with how we travel, dress, furnish our homes, shop, are entertained, and otherwise pamper ourselves. What we save from cutting corners — from the practice of mindful fasting — may amaze us. From those saved resources we might find we can give more generously than we ever could before for the sake of those whose poverty would also amaze us, if we were to notice it.

And so it seems quite appropriate that Jesus now turns our attention from these three acts of piety to a lengthy discussion of riches, righteousness, and anxiety.

11

Riches, Righteousness, and Anxiety

—⟨∞⟩—

6:19"Do not lay up for yourselves treasures on earth, where moth and rust consume and where thieves break in and steal, 20but lay up for yourselves treasures in heaven, where neither moth nor rust consumes and where thieves do not break in and steal. 21For where your treasure is, there will your heart be also. 22The eye is the lamp of the body. So, if your eye is sound, your whole body will be full of light; 23but if your eye is not sound, your whole body will be full of darkness. If then the light in you is darkness, how great is the darkness! 24No one can serve two masters; for either he will hate the one and love the other, or he will be devoted to the one and despise the other. You cannot serve God and mammon. 25Therefore I tell you, do not be anxious about your life, what you shall eat or what you shall drink, nor about your body, what you shall put on. Is not life more than food, and the body more than clothing? 26Look at the birds of the air: they neither sow nor reap nor gather into barns, and yet your heavenly Father feeds them. Are you not of more value than they? 27And which of you by being anxious can add one cubit to his span of life? 28And why are you anxious about clothing?

Consider the lilies of the field, how they grow; they neither toil nor spin; [29]yet I tell you, even Solomon in all his glory was not arrayed like one of these. [30]But if God so clothes the grass of the field, which today is alive and tomorrow is thrown into the oven, will he not much more clothe you, O men of little faith? [31]Therefore do not be anxious, saying, 'What shall we eat?' or 'What shall we drink?' or 'What shall we wear?' [32]For the Gentiles seek all these things; and your heavenly Father knows that you need them all. [33]But seek first his kingdom and his righteousness, and all these things shall be yours as well. [34]Therefore do not be anxious about tomorrow, for tomorrow will be anxious for itself. Let the day's own trouble be sufficient for the day."

What follows from this point on in the Sermon is an elaboration of themes we have already encountered. In some particulars, the passage above appears to pick up on petitions in the Lord's Prayer and expand on them. There are four key lines, those around which the rest of the passage may be said to "cluster." I present them here in notebook style as "four points":

1. *Be focused on the right goal:* "The eye is the lamp of the body. So, if your eye is sound [literally, *haplous* = 'single'], your whole body will be full of light; but if your eye is not sound ['single'], your whole body will be full of darkness. If then the light in you is darkness, how great is the darkness!"

2. *Serve God with undivided intent:* "No one can serve two masters; for either he will hate the one and love the other, or he will be devoted to the one and despise the other. You cannot serve God and mammon."

3. *Resolve not to give in to anxiety:* "Do not be anxious about your life. . . . Therefore do not be anxious, saying, 'What shall we eat?' or 'What shall we drink?' or 'What shall we wear?' . . . Therefore do not be anxious about tomorrow, for tomorrow

will be anxious for itself. Let the day's own trouble be sufficient for the day."

4. *Make "seeking the kingdom" (i.e., living life according to its ways
= God's "righteousness") your priority:* "But seek first his kingdom and his righteousness, and all these things [i.e., the
things you really need] shall be yours as well."

The four points are connected logically in this way:

- First, we can choose where we will put our focus in life. We can
choose either the light of the kingdom and of God, or the relative darkness of lesser pursuits.
- Second, God should be the master of our life's direction, and
we should follow him with undivided mind, or "purity of
heart" (5:8). To do this is to "see" clearly and thus to be filled
with the "light" mentioned in verses 22-23.
- Third, if we have an unhealthy obsession with lesser concerns,
which is the temptation whenever we aren't satisfied with
what we need and already have in sufficiency, it will make us
anxious, worried, and stressed. Anxiety is the counterproduc-
tive expenditure of our energy and inner peace, and it is the
antithesis of faith. To be anxious is, in other words, one of the
things that fills us with the interior "darkness" of the analogy
above, and is what is meant by "serving Mammon."
- Fourth, therefore, our priority in life should be clear to us: it is
to seek first God's kingdom and righteousness (the "light"), to
serve him instead of "Mammon," and to let this kingdom and
righteousness satisfy us and banish our anxieties.

This whole section of the Sermon begins with the subject of
material accumulation. As we noted in the preceding chapter,
Westerners live in a culture of consumerism. We are inundated by
it. Almost every component of modern culture is geared to sell us
something, from sedans to soap to sound systems to sex. If we

want it, it can be bought; if we don't want it, the media will still try to sell us on the line that we can't live without it. Our eyes and ears are stuffed with advertising, our lust for possessions is kept artificially stimulated to fever pitch, and we go through our lives wanting more, more, more.

The world in which Jesus lived was divided between the very wealthy and the very poor. Archaeological discoveries in the Holy Land have revealed that life in that age, especially in cities like Jerusalem, could be very luxurious. Consumerism existed then as now, there as here, and Jesus would have seen instances of immense affluence right alongside sights of extreme destitution. So what Jesus says was as relevant then as it is today. He gives us a sharp division which runs right through this section. It's a clear either/or ethic. We can *either* accumulate material treasure, allowing our lives to be consumed by the stuff we consume and burdened by the sheer amassing of the things we hoard, which are always under threat of being destroyed, squandered, or stolen; *or* we can direct our sights and efforts toward the coming kingdom and God's will being done "on earth as in heaven." We can *either* serve "Mammon" — a word that reflects a half-forgotten mythological personification of riches and avarice, and indicates a sort of life tangled up with things and money and their attendant worries — *or* we can serve God.

"Treasure" laid up in heaven means, quite simply, the fruit of lives of compassion and care that we are responsible for cultivating here on earth for the sake of others, a treasure which can be said to be amassed and kept for us "in heaven" because it is the bringing about of God's will "on earth *as it is in heaven.*" Treasure is laid up "in heaven" whenever it is generously shared among others here on earth. It is akin to the idea of forgiving others' debts and thereby having our own forgiven in turn. It is, in practice, the mutual distribution that should be common between disciples — fellow disciples share with us, we share with them, and our needs should be met in mutual care. Such sharing should reach out beyond the circle of the community of disciples and into the world and to those in need.

Jesus was not a capitalist. He didn't promote competition or getting rich at the expense of others. Any creation of wealth should be for the common good — not merely for individual, familial, or commercial gain. When describing the common life of the first Christians, the book of Acts puts it this way: "Now the company of those who believed were of one heart and soul, and no one said that any of the things which he possessed was his own, but they had everything in common [*koina*]" (Acts 4:32). Paul expressed this same principle of mutuality: "Bear one another's burdens, and so fulfill the law of Christ" (Gal. 6:2).

Our treasure, therefore, is for sharing, and sharing is what creates *koinonia* ("common life," "participation," "partnership") = *communio* = "fellowship." But treasure, whether money or property, laid up only "on earth" — that is, only for our own indulgence, buried within the "earth" of our exclusive wants and self-interest (which is the meaning of "Mammon," or avarice) — will always carry with it the seeds of anxiety. Perhaps my possessions will be damaged or destroyed. Perhaps they will be stolen or swallowed up in an unwise investment. And — no "perhaps" about this one — when I die, they won't mean anything to me anymore anyway. I'll be dead, my body will rot, and nothing I owned will really have warranted the many hours and restless busyness I spent on getting it.

Jesus uses two analogies to drive home the points that we need to focus on what we really should be pursuing, and to pursue that with singleness of purpose. The first analogy — that of eyesight — is a bit obscure for us moderns. But the gist is easy enough to understand. The eyes were considered "windows" that let light into the body. Obviously, in darkness, light could not stream in, nor could it come in if the window was blurred or blinded. Jesus' meaning is that our eyes should be "sound" or "healthy." The Greek word, as I've already noted, means "single."

The implication is that one must be focused on a *single aim,* and that a person cannot be focused on more than one object at a time and see clearly.

In a spiritual sense, attempting to focus on more than one goal leaves one not only with double vision, but also with "double-mindedness," a condition that is decried in the Epistle of James in two places. (James in particular echoes many of the points and phrases found in the Sermon on the Mount.) In James 1:7-8, we read, "A double-minded man, unstable in all his ways, will [not] receive anything from the Lord." These verses are immediately followed by a contrast of "the lowly" and "the rich." Again, in 4:8, we read, "Draw near to God and he will draw near to you. Cleanse your hands, you sinners, and purify your hearts, you men of double mind." Singleness of sight and singleness of mind mean setting ourselves on the way of Jesus, clearly distinguishing what that way *is* and what it is *not* (see Matt. 7:13-14 below), and sticking to that way without getting sidetracked or confused about the destination.

It's always tempting to think we can do two things at the same time, that Jesus' way and the world's way or our way can somehow be made into one way after all, that there really is no hard choice to make. So it is, for example, that we might fool ourselves into believing it right to support the latest "just war" and yet be following Jesus, or to link God and country into an inseparable and sacred idol, or to accumulate and amass and set ourselves up for a safe and secure old age while neglecting our support of others. . . . The list could go on and on. Whenever we opt for our own personal peace and security at any expense, without realizing that we're never likely to achieve either fully, we are becoming double-minded and losing our focus. We are serving "Mammon."

The second analogy, then, has to do with serving or slavery. Indeed, the word for "serve" is *douleuein,* and it means "to slave." To become God's "slaves" means to render voluntary service to him, to give ourselves to his guidance and care. We can offer ourselves to God or to Mammon. But, whichever we choose, we really cannot choose both. Jesus doesn't allow us to mix our motives. Either we will love and devote ourselves to God, hating and despising Mammon; or we will love and be devoted to Mammon, and hate and despise God. Even if we have no awareness that we have become double-minded on the level of theoretical accommodation, in practice we have. In our world there are far more practical atheists who think they are religious than there are theoretically doctrinaire atheists.

Verses 25-34 are quite straightforward and need little comment. One can read and re-read them both for the challenge they provide and for the beauty of the words. Jesus' use of natural imagery reminds us of his great joy in the earthly beauty he saw. Birds and flowers become our exemplars. Jesus speaks not only as a prophet but also as a poet. These words are supremely comforting, reminding us that God knows our needs and we have no need to worry.

But they are only comforting up to a point.

We are told that God provides for our needs, for instance, not our wants. He knows we need food, drink, and clothes. We are told not to worry about tomorrow — each day brings its own troubles, and we must deal with them as they come. In other words, we will not have a trouble-free existence. But worrying and fretting about the future should not characterize us.

If we're preoccupied with our future "personal peace and security," then we're inviting anxiety and straying from our priority of putting God's kingdom and righteousness first in our daily living. If, let's say, we're sucked up into fears of a coming "tribulation," looking for signs of the Antichrist, and counting the days till the "end times," we are squandering our time and ignoring the kingdom we're supposed to be inviting into our lives each day through our actions. If we're unduly worried about the survival of American values or Western civilization, we're depending on the survival of a temporal and temporary reality and not on the kingdom that has no beginning or end. And if we worry about our own death or the death of those we love, well . . . that is inevitable and natural, and it is something worthy of our deep meditation. If we trust God for each day of our life, we must learn to trust him about the last day we will ever have. That eventuality we must simply leave to him.

This is one of those portions in the Sermon that is most often quoted. It is usually seen as a comfort, a calming of our fears, a few inspirational words of tranquility. The truth, of course, is that these words are bracing and urge us to examine our hearts and motives more closely.

12

"Judge Not!"

———◦◦◦———

The remainder of the Sermon on the Mount continues with Jesus' directives to his disciples regarding their life in community with one another. The church that Jesus envisions is one made up of bands of disciples living and sharing an alternative existence in the midst of a society ruled by a very different sort of kingdom. Matthew's Gospel is the only one that uses the word we usually translate as "church" (16:18; 18:17). In Jesus' Rome-dominated world, the term *ecclesia* normally referred to a political assembly. In the ancient Greek translation of the Old Testament, this word is used for the whole "assembly" (*qahal* in Hebrew) of Israel. The word, then, has both political and religious significance, and in this culture the two were not so easily separated as "church" and "state" have become in our more secular age.

Jesus used politically charged language simply by using the word *basileia,* which means "kingdom" or "empire." When he also said that the empire he was introducing into the world is that "of God" (= "heaven"), he rhetorically trumped the claims of Rome. They had their false gods, but Jesus claimed the authority of the one, only God. Caesar claimed to be a son of a (false) god; Jesus claimed that the living God was his Father. What's more, he claimed that all his disciples could claim God as their Father, too. God is "*our* Father."

Jesus' empire or kingdom is thus a political-religious society, an assembly (*ecclesia* = "church") of equals gathered about God and his "Messiah" ("Anointed One" = "Christ"), who is the one Rabbi and Teacher among these disciples. "And you are not to be called rabbi, for you have one teacher, and you are all brethren. And call no man your father on earth, for you have one Father, who is in heaven. Neither be called masters, for you have one master, the Christ" (Matt. 23:8-10). Jesus teaches a way that will do two things: transform his disciples' lives spiritually from within, and create a visible society of love, peace, and righteousness.

It can't be denied that the record of the church's history is checkered at best, and that great good has often been countered and occasionally overwhelmed by great evil — all done in the name of Jesus. Nevertheless, to the extent that the standards of Western civilization are charitable, open to reform, and influential in promoting equality and justice, we have Christianity to thank. Those who see the church as having been only a force for oppression, backwardness, decadence, and even worse things are either ignorant of history or else being willfully disingenuous.

Still, there is no doubt but that those who follow Jesus need to be renewed in every age by recourse to Jesus' original vision. How might we appropriate his political-religious kingdom today, in our own circumstances? Can we form communities of disciples who are open to living and learning from Jesus directly, so to speak? Perhaps we have a greater chance today, as institutional structures and old ecclesiastical bureaucracies begin to crumble, no longer propped up by supposedly "Christian" governments and nations, to rethink and imaginatively create new ways of living as Jesus' disciples.

For that vision, we have a series of sayings in the remaining portions of the Sermon which directly address how we live and learn together in community. They deal with how we are to interact among ourselves, how we are to pass on Jesus' teachings with discernment, how we are to rely on God together in prayer, and just how seriously we are to regard the distinction between living the way of Jesus and living the way of the world (the latter being exemplified by the brutal, authoritarian, imperialistic, and militaristic government of Rome).

Jesus' first words in this respect, then, are an injunction against being judges of one another:

> *7:1 "Judge not, that you be not judged. 2For with the judgment you pronounce you will be judged, and the measure you give will be the measure you get. 3Why do you see the speck that is in your brother's eye, but do not notice the log that is in your own eye? 4Or how can you say to your brother, 'Let me take the speck out of your eye,' when there is the log in your own eye? 5You hypocrite, first take the log out of your own eye, and then you will see clearly to take the speck out of your brother's eye."*

A passage in the Epistle of James picks up on this theme, as it does so many others in the Sermon on the Mount, and helps to spell out Jesus' meaning here:

> Do not speak evil against one another, brethren. He that speaks evil against a brother or judges his brother, speaks evil against the law and judges the law. But if you judge the law, you are not a doer of the law but a judge. There is one lawgiver and judge, he who is able to save and to destroy. But who are you that you judge your neighbor? (James 4:11-12)

Here it is worth noticing that James equates "judging" another with "speaking evil against another." The two go hand in hand, thus ruling out gossip, for instance. "Speaking evil" may not be anything too derogatory in nature, just a bit critical, just a little jaundiced, just a tad dismissive of another. Or it can be out-and-out slander. Whenever we set about analyzing another, we become judges of the law itself. The Torah, as Jesus teaches it, tells us that insulting someone or calling someone a fool puts us on the slippery slope to judgment, being in effect in violation of the commandment "You shall not kill" (Matt. 5:21-22). James very pointedly reminds us that "there is one lawgiver and judge" — and we're not him!

Paul, in response to those who were taking it upon themselves to judge him, wrote much the same:

> But with me it is a very small thing that I should be judged by you or by any human court. I do not even judge myself. I am not aware of anything against myself, but I am not thereby acquitted. It is the Lord who judges me. Therefore do not pronounce judgment before the time, before the Lord comes, who will bring to light the things now hidden in darkness and will disclose the purposes of the heart. Then every man will receive his commendation from God. (1 Cor. 4:3-5)

Again, Paul reminds his readers that only God is the judge, not us. He even dares not to judge himself, he tells us, since God knows him better than he knows himself. (It goes without saying that Paul made this statement ages before anyone had ever spoken of a "subconscious" mind.) He knows that God sees those winding passageways and inner caverns of the heart's depths, an area of the human soul which we only glimpse from time to time, and which not infrequently startles us when a true light of perception is shone unexpectedly into this or that dark crevice. We can get a jolt sometimes when we are allowed to see what really lurks inside us. We might well say that such moments are just between our selves and God, and that we need no third party to see our dreariest or dirtiest thoughts laid bare — that it's none of their business. But if that's the case with us, it should likewise be the case for others in our estimation. We cannot know our deepest selves all that well, except in dribs and drabs, so how can we presume to "know" others any better? That's God's business, not ours — whether dealing with ourselves or with others. We should leave it to God, then, and say nothing about another in judgment. We should believe that God is dealing adequately enough with that individual.

Jesus' words remind us that if we judge another, God will judge us accordingly. If we are harsh critics of another, God will be a harsh critic of us. If we treat others with graciousness and patience, God will likewise treat us graciously and patiently.

Another way we might read these verses, however, is to see something a bit "karmic" in them. In other words, we may find ourselves reaping what we have sown (Gal. 6:7). God may not *directly* judge us with harshness if we judge others harshly ourselves. Nonetheless, *indirectly* his judgment may be felt in how others react to us. Notice the imprecision of Jesus' words, his avoidance of saying anything about God's *direct* judgment: "Judge not, that you be not judged. For with the judgment you pronounce you will be judged, and the measure you give will be the measure you get." There is something subtle here in how Jesus speaks of the judgment we get back for judging others — whether through gossip, criticism, or condemnation. It might be the sort of judgment in which "what goes around comes around" — others may treat us as we have treated them. Possibly this lies behind the warning in the Epistle to the Hebrews that the community should "see to it . . . that no 'root of bitterness' spring up and cause trouble, and by it the many become defiled" (Heb. 12:15). When we speak judgmentally of others, critically or disdainfully, it is often only a matter of time before we find the same coming back in our direction. Bitterness can very easily and quickly take root in a community, and it rapidly defiles "the many." Whole communities suffer and sometimes dissolve precisely because of such undisciplined internal criticism between members.

But what if we see a fault in another which we know legitimately needs correction? Jesus warns us that, if we really wish to help another, we had best be sure we see clearly enough to do him good and not harm. It's doubtful that any of us would wish to receive eye surgery at the hands of a blind eye surgeon. That's the idea behind Jesus' suggestion that we get our own eyes cleared of obstructions before we stick our fingers into someone else's eye to help get a splinter out. That we should try to do such a delicate operation with a log jammed in our own eye only heightens the absurdity of this intentionally absurd analogy (is the "log" to be understood as our propensity to judge another — thus giving us an idea of how disproportionate our own fault of judging another is in comparison to our neighbor's fault, whatever it might be?).

The conclusion Jesus draws is that we can help others, once we have dealt with our own areas of blindness and incomprehension first. We must be disciples, not judges, not prone to gossip or criticism, willing to let others develop in their own ways without our interference, before we ever presume to help others deal with their faults and failures.

Lastly, it is again a matter of practicing detachment. This is, in fact, part of the inner discipline we must study to perfect: not to look at others critically, but to accept them without too many expectations or any irritations (often two sides of the same coin). Apart from obvious, gross, and destructive behavior in the community of disciples (for which Jesus outlines a corrective procedure in Matthew 18), one should focus on one's own spiritual and moral life as a disciple. We are not called to police our neighbor or sit in judgment of anyone else. We are called to exercise charity and mercy, patience and long-suffering. We are to treat others with respect and honor, as children of the same Father who are also learning the way of Jesus in common with ourselves.

According to the Gospel of John, when Peter became too nosy about the plans Jesus had for another disciple, Jesus turned and said to him, "If it is my will that he [the other disciple] remain until I come, what is that to you? Follow me! [literally, '*You* follow me!']" (John 21:22).

The message is unmistakable: as a general rule of thumb we ought to keep our eyes on Jesus and not on others. And further, unless it's requested of us, we should let others do the same without our "helpful" interference.

13

Dogs and Holy Things and Pigs and Pearls

———— ✥ ————

I mmediately after Jesus' injunction against judging others, we have this jarring word that apparently — if not directly, at least in temper — contradicts the former saying:

> 7:6 *"Do not give dogs what is holy; and do not throw your pearls before swine, lest they trample them under foot and turn to attack you."*

The closest we come in this same Gospel to such a sentiment as this can be found in two later passages. The first of these comes from Jesus' discourse to his disciples, in which he tells them how they should go about proclaiming the message of the kingdom. If they and the message are received, well and good; but if they are not, says Jesus, the rejected disciples are to "shake off the dust from your feet as you leave that house or town. Truly, I say to you, it shall be more tolerable on the day of judgment for the land of Sodom and Gomorrah than for that town" (Matt. 10:14-15).

Jesus speaks here as a prophet, underlining the urgency of his message. This was a commonplace for prophetic utterance, something which was presented as a message from God and therefore of utmost importance for the hearers. We have to accept Jesus' prophetic manner of speaking as part and parcel of the cultural context in which he lived and operated. This may not sit well with "politically correct" modern sensibilities, but Jesus was not speaking primarily to us. He was speaking to first-century Palestinian Jews, and this was the language they understood. (For further discussion on Matthew's emphasis on the theme of judgment, see Appendix 2.)

The same may be said of the even more disturbing words of Jesus in Matthew 15:21-28, in which he refers to a Gentile woman and her demon-possessed daughter as "dogs." I quote the passage here in full:

> And Jesus went away from there and withdrew to the district of Tyre and Sidon. And behold, a Canaanite woman from that region came out and cried, "Have mercy on me, O Lord, Son of David; my daughter is severely possessed by a demon." But he did not answer her a word. And his disciples came and begged him, saying, "Send her away, for she is crying after us." He answered, "I was sent only to the lost sheep of the house of Israel." But she came and knelt before him, saying, "Lord, help me." And he answered, "It is not fair to take the children's bread and throw it to the dogs." She said, "Yes, Lord, yet even the dogs eat the crumbs that fall from their master's table." Then Jesus answered her, "O woman, great is your faith! Be it done for you as you desire." And her daughter was healed instantly.

I must say that, as a Gentile, I may not have been as persistent as this woman proved to be in getting Jesus' aid after such an unnecessary rebuff. Or would I? If it was my own daughter, perhaps I would have humbled myself as utterly as she did and begged his help, even if it meant being insulted in the process. *And that is in fact precisely the point of the passage.* In this incident, context is everything.

And the context is this. It has to do with a contrast. In the preceding passage — 15:1-20 — Jesus had just had a major clash with the Pharisees and scribes, his own people's most revered religious authorities, who had come from "headquarters" in Jerusalem precisely to grill him. Jesus had given them an earful, lambasting their hypocrisy and leaving them smarting. Immediately following this incident, we read, "Then the disciples came and said to him, 'Do you know that the Pharisees were offended when they heard this saying?' He answered, 'Every plant which my heavenly Father has not planted will be rooted up. Let them alone; they are blind guides. And if a blind man leads a blind man, both will fall into a pit'" (vv. 12-14). Then, *in the very next passage,* he is approached by the Gentile woman. He rebuffs her, she pleads for help nonetheless, and — ultimately, and before the eyes of his disciples — he holds her up as *an example of faith.* Jesus' commendation of her faith, in other words, is meant to stand in contrast to his denunciation of the hypocrisy of the scribes and Pharisees.

In other words, the Pharisees are revealed as "blind," although they worship the God of Israel, whom Jesus represents; but a persistent and daring woman of another people and a different religion is graciously shown the light, even though she would normally have been considered by the likes of those so recently upbraided by Jesus as religiously blind herself, not deserving of God's attention, and no better than a "dog" (a common pejorative term for Gentiles). The lesson could not be clearer, the contrast more striking. There is neither an "anti-Gentile" lesson on the one hand nor an "anti-Semitic" lesson on the other in the juxtaposition of these passages; rather, doggedness (if you will pardon the pun), not overconfidence, is what is highlighted as the right approach to God by the contrast they demonstrate in context. What is *not* decisive is one's ethnicity or even religious "correctness" (the latter being something the official church has too often forgotten during its history).

With this in mind, let's return to Matthew 7:6. Who are the

"dogs" and "swine" in Jesus' saying? It's safe to say that he isn't referring to Gentiles with such unflattering language. Nor is he contradicting his own teaching on judging others. Let's take the second possible objection first. Jesus' words regarding judgment have to do with the internal life of the community of his disciples, as we have noted. Nonetheless, there is no implied permission here for anyone to judge those outside the community, either. The references to "dogs" and "swine" in this saying are in fact not used pejoratively of anybody in particular at all.

These terms refer to spiritual *attitudes,* not persons. This is the perennial language of a spiritual master, and it is something that can be found in wisdom traditions universally. Unless a person comes to a spiritual master with the properly receptive attitude — that is, with the right disposition of teachableness and humility — the master will customarily withhold spiritual teaching. A time of testing should precede taking on anyone who says he or she wants to be a disciple. Willingness to listen attentively is a prerequisite for discipleship. Mere inquisitiveness is not enough. Neither is an attitude of argumentativeness and resistance. It's one thing to ask questions, to seek answers, to press on with perseverance until one has grasped something valuable in the quest for spiritual wisdom and inner transformation. It's another to come with preconceived ideas, a half-baked agenda, or a manner of haughtiness or superciliousness.

Jesus makes this distinction later in the same Gospel when he discusses the role his parables play:

> Then the disciples came and said to him, "Why do you speak to them in parables?" And he answered them, "To you it has been given to know the secrets of the kingdom of heaven, but to them it has not been given. For to him who has will more be given, and he will have abundance; but from him who has not, even what he has will be taken away. This is why I speak to them in parables, because seeing they do not see, and hearing they do

not hear, nor do they understand. With them indeed is fulfilled the prophecy of Isaiah which says: 'You shall indeed hear but never understand, and you shall indeed see but never perceive. For this people's heart has grown dull, and their ears are heavy of hearing, and their eyes they have closed, lest they should perceive with their eyes, and hear with their ears, and understand with their heart, and turn for me to heal them.' But blessed are your eyes, for they see, and your ears, for they hear. Truly, I say to you, many prophets and righteous men longed to see what you see, and did not see it, and to hear what you hear, and did not hear it." (Matt. 13:10-17; cf. Isa. 6:9-10)

In this saying Jesus makes a distinction between those *inside* and those *outside* his community of disciples. The parables — stories with meanings that required attentiveness, interest, and pursuit for understanding — acted as both a curtain between the two groups and an enticement to those seeking knowledge of the kingdom of heaven to press into and beyond. To those within, to his dedicated disciples, Jesus gives his "secrets."

"Holy things" and "pearls" are terms that are used in our saying from the Sermon to refer to these "secrets" — the teachings of the kingdom. "Dogs" and "swine" refer to persons' *attitudes of disrespect* for the sacred, derisive of wisdom, which many exhibit. Jesus says that until those with such "doggish" or "swinish" dispositions have a change of heart, they shouldn't be invited within the community of disciples. Some sort of testing (a practice of the early church for a number of generations before the empire became "Christianized," and being "Christian" in name only became a real problem) should be carried out before letting anyone in fully.

If ever there were a saying of Jesus long disused and neglected, this is certainly it. All we need to do is consider how so much that is sacred in Christianity has become openly known, ridiculed, and only partially understood at best by those most likely to dismiss it out of hand. It is true that Christians are most to blame for this situation. Because they were unable to restrict their teachings to those most ready to receive them earnestly, these teachings have been bandied about publicly for centuries. What were words of wisdom to be pondered and translated into contemplation and action were turned into theological formulas and anathemas. What had been mysteries that worked deeply and transformatively in the hearers were reduced to dry systems, with ever more technical and philosophical language heaped on for good measure. From systems came arguments, confusion, greater fine-tuning, condemnations of those who didn't subscribe to the "correct" interpretations of these dry concepts, and eventually persecution of those individuals. And, as the power of the institutions that wielded these systems eventually waned, the ridicule of such abuse of intellect and the spirit grew stronger, and those wanting to escape from it multiplied. What was rejected was not Jesus himself; but those doing the rejecting didn't always know that. They were fleeing something massive, oppressive, repressive, and largely unrecognizable as reflective of Jesus himself. They left behind what had become absurd in their eyes. Holy things and pearls had been cast before the most "doggish" and "swinish" attitudes of mind for far too long, and there was a trampling of them underfoot. One can't blame the "dogs" or the "swine" for this; the blame lies with those who flung their holy things and pearls in the mud before them.

It's time we reclaimed this wise saying. Our post-Christian culture may very well give us the opportunity to relearn the wisdom of doing so. Communities of followers of Jesus may grow smaller, commitment to his teachings more radical and real, and in time we may look like those with something valuable that others want and will seek to have. That will happen as we become more spiritually deep and more seriously active in our discipleship, both as individuals and as communities.

Prayer and the Golden Rule

━━━∽∾∽━━━

7:7 "Ask, and it will be given you; seek, and you will find; knock, and it will be opened to you. 8For every one who asks receives, and he who seeks finds, and to him who knocks it will be opened. 9Or what man of you, if his son asks him for bread, will give him a stone? 10Or if he asks for a fish, will give him a serpent? 11If you then, who are evil, know how to give good gifts to your children, how much more will your Father who is in heaven give good things to those who ask him! 12So whatever you wish that men would do to you, do so to them; for this is the law and the prophets."

Just as Jesus followed his teaching of what has come to be called the Lord's Prayer with an exhortation to forgive (see 6:14-15 above), so here, when once more he comes to the subject of prayer, he immediately follows it with an exhortation to do good to others. The link between prayer and practice is never forgotten. The two must always be joined. Prayer without practice — like faith without works — is dead (see James 2:17).

As with the first six verses of Chapter 7, these verses are directed to the daily exercising of communal life. Jesus envisions a community of disciples who — as we have just seen — do not judge and backbite one another (thus maintaining harmony among themselves), who guard from desecration the teaching and principles by which they live (thus letting their lives, not their dogmas, speak for themselves and hence win over others), and — as we now see — who pray and work together.

Visible in these pithy words are the unusual and sharp images Jesus employs to make his arguments. In inviting his disciples to pray for "good things" from their Father, he summons up the unlikely and unlovely pictures of a man giving his son, who asks him for food, a stone instead of bread and a serpent instead of a fish. It's a perverse or mad man who would do any such thing, and the image it conjures up reminds the reader of the sort of character that might inhabit Alice's Looking-Glass World.

Jesus says that, even though we are all *poneroi* — "morally bad persons" (translated "evil" here) — we still know how to give appropriate gifts to our children. Morally bad people still do good things for those they love. Jesus uses the "If you then . . . how much more" style of argument, moving from the lesser to the greater. If human beings, as bad as they can be, can nevertheless do good, how much more will the One who is goodness itself give "good things" to those who crave them?

Jesus doesn't place the emphasis on our propensity to do evil. He never harangues us about such an obvious human tendency. He merely assumes quite realistically the ambivalence in our moral condition. On the contrary, he emphasizes the goodness of God, who provides for the children for whom he cares. As we have seen, he cares for the good and the evil, the just and the unjust, providing sunshine and rain to all indifferently. But, of course, the "good things" Jesus refers to in this passage are of a higher order than those most basic of heavenly provisions, and those who here "ask, seek, and knock" for them are those who know God to be their loving Father. The message is that they can trust him to give them what they need.

The "good things" spoken of here, we can surmise, are the things requested in the invocations of the Lord's Prayer — the coming of the kingdom, the accomplishment on earth of God's will (through the community of disciples), the supply necessary for our physical welfare, the forgiveness of our debts (with the grace to forgive others theirs), and deliverance from the sort of evil that condemns our lives to misery and guilt. Other good things may be the provision of an ever-increasing experiential knowledge of God, or of greater capacity to love others and to do good works, or of peace, and so forth.

That these "good things" are of a spiritual order, meant to transform our characters and minds — and not, for instance, requests for material acquisitions — is suggested by how Luke translates the same statement in his version. Matthew has "how much more will your Father who is in heaven give *good things* to those who ask him!"; Luke has "how much more will the heavenly Father give *the Holy Spirit* to those who ask him!" (Luke 11:13, emphasis mine). For Luke, all good things come by way of the gift of the Holy Spirit (literally, "Holy Breath") of God. Prayer, then, is for acquiring what helps us become a city set on a hill, the salt of the earth, the light of the world. It is always an opening up of our selves to God, a broadening of mind and heart, a transfiguration of our souls, a deepening of understanding and peace with God and all things and all people.

"So [or 'therefore']," concludes Jesus, "whatever you wish that men would do to you, do so to them; for this is the law and the prophets." Once more, we are reminded that Jesus has come to fulfill the law and the prophets, and therefore the Sermon on the Mount is an interpretation and a universalizing of the Torah. He gives the "Golden Rule," which is found in both positive ("Do . . .") and negative ("Do not . . .") forms in virtually every culture and religion in the world. Jesus is not professing to be original. He would have known this teaching from the synagogue as part of his upbringing. But here he makes it the linchpin of all his ethical doctrine. It applies both to those within and to those outside the community, as the entire Sermon up to this point makes abundantly clear.

The form he chooses for expressing it is the proactive one of "doing." Once again we are reminded of the essential pragmatism of Jesus' message and kingdom. We do good works so that the world can see God active in us, and praise the Father (5:16).

We come full circle here, and in one sense this concludes the Sermon on the Mount. However, Jesus has more to say, and he has saved his most biting words for us for the conclusion. What follows now is a teaching about the teaching itself: How seriously will we take it to heart? Everything, Jesus will tell us, depends on that. If you will be my disciples, he will in effect ask us, are you ready to take this yoke upon your shoulders or not? If you assume it, you will be expected to carry it to the end.

It isn't a philosophy to be taken up lightly, nor is it a smorgasbord of good advice. Picking and choosing from it is not invited. In fact, in no uncertain terms, Jesus will make the point that his teaching is crucial and requires single-mindedness. You can go one way or another, but there must inevitably be a dividing of the ways — and that fork in the road exists within our deepest selves.

The Parting of the Ways

7:13 "Enter by the narrow gate; for the gate is wide and the way is easy, that leads to destruction, and those who enter by it are many. 14For the gate is narrow and the way is hard, that leads to life, and those who find it are few. 15Beware of false prophets, who come to you in sheep's clothing but inwardly are ravenous wolves. 16You will know them by their fruits. Are grapes gathered from thorns, or figs from thistles? 17So, every sound tree bears good fruit, but the bad tree bears evil fruit. 18A sound tree cannot bear evil fruit, nor can a bad tree bear good fruit. 19Every tree that does not bear good fruit is cut down and thrown into the fire. 20Thus you will know them by their fruits. 21Not every one who says to me, 'Lord, Lord,' shall enter the kingdom of heaven, but he who does the will of my Father who is in heaven. 22On that day many will say to me, 'Lord, Lord, did we not prophesy in your name, and cast out demons in your name, and do many mighty works in your name?' 23And then will I declare to them, 'I never knew you; depart from me, you evildoers.' 24Every one then who hears these words of mine and does them will be like a wise man who built his house upon the rock; 25and the rain fell, and the

floods came, and the winds blew and beat upon that house,
but it did not fall, because it had been founded on the rock.
[26]And every one who hears these words of mine and does not
do them will be like a foolish man who built his house upon
the sand; [27]and the rain fell, and the floods came, and the
winds blew and beat against that house, and it fell; and great
was the fall of it."

Jesus concludes the Sermon with three sets of contrary images: the narrow gate and way and the wide gate and way; the sound tree that bears good fruit and the bad tree that bears evil fruit; and the house built on a foundation of rock and the house built on a foundation of sand.

Along with these main, guiding images are two important secondary images: a portrayal of "false prophets" as "wolves in sheep's clothing," whom Jesus warns against; and a corresponding depiction of those who had formerly called Jesus "Lord" during their lives, but had not done as he said, and are now described as abjectly pleading before him on the "day" of judgment. The latter can be assumed to be the same as the wolfish "false prophets" mentioned above — those commissioned with spiritual authority, and who are even described as having prophesied, cast out demons, and done mighty works in Jesus' name.

This account of their apparently very real activities, all of them sensational and even miraculous in nature, reveals that Jesus did not place any great or determinative weight on the performance of such astounding works by his followers. Despite the fact that the Gospels abound with Jesus' own mighty deeds, there is little in his words to suggest that the miraculous should have much emphasis among his disciples. Indeed, as we have already seen and shall yet see, Jesus puts adherence to his way of life, God's kingdom and righteousness, and his ethics and interpretation of the Torah far above anything like "supernatural" showmanship. Those who in this passage are depicted as claiming *to have done* all sorts of marvelous things in Jesus' name, thereby giving him the credit, but *have also not done* "the will of my Father who is in heaven" (that is, charitable works — see again 5:16), are dismissed with the harrowing words "I never knew you; depart from me, you evildoers." The irony, of course, is that those asserting that they have powerfully done his will, invoking him as "Lord," are declared by him to be virtual strangers. A more harsh and critical retort can scarcely be imagined.

So we see that two classes of disciples are issued warnings in this concluding passage. Those commissioned with authority and tasks of guidance and healing for the community are forewarned to live up to the "greater righteousness" Jesus requires from his followers (cf. 5:20). But Jesus is not only concerned with those who have oversight in the community; it is clear that he intends the same admonition for all his disciples. After all, as Jesus teaches and as we have already noted, all are really equals in his kingdom. Essentially there are no "greater" or "lesser" persons among his brothers and sisters. "Clergy" are not a separate order of human being than "laity" — "clergy" are merely those selected laypersons who are assigned tasks of serving the other disciples in various ways (taking the lead in worship, teaching, proclaiming, and doing works of charity). But all are God's children. Everything depends on Jesus' disciples both *listening* to him and *doing* as he instructs — not just listening, approving, and then continuing to live as they please. Everyone is to pass through the same gate, to travel the same way, to be a sound tree bearing good fruit, and to build for himself or herself a house on a solid foundation.

Dealing first with the false prophets, we should understand the term "prophets" to refer to any who speak to the community of disciples in God's or Jesus' name. There will be some who are "ravenous wolves," probably meaning those who use their "prophesying" as a means to line their own pockets, or — as the old analogy has it — to fleece the sheep. We have all seen it. Dishonest and manipulative priests, preachers, evangelists, "prophets," and pastors, employing their power, positions, dramatic skills, voices, and even undoubted charismatic gifts (whether natural or preternatural, who can tell?) — they have plagued the Christian world since the days of Simon Magus (see Acts 8). They come, says Jesus, looking like fellow "sheep," but — shifting analogies — like healthy or sick trees, they can be known by the quality of their fruits.

How could early disciples discern these revealing "fruits"? One ancient text, nearly as old as — or, as some scholars have suggested, even older than — Matthew's Gospel, clues us in as to how this might have been done within early Christian circles. Indeed, the same ancient text was written for Christians in Syria, and possibly even for the same Syrian communities for whom Matthew's Gospel was composed. Be that as it may, this ancient rule book for Christian communal life, known as *The Didache* (or, *The Teaching of the Twelve Apostles*), quite possibly written sometime between A.D. 50 and 150, gives such directions as these regarding those claiming to be prophets:

> Not everyone who speaks in spirit is a prophet, except he have the behavior of the Lord. From his behavior, then, the false prophet and the true prophet shall be known. . . . And every prophet who teaches the truth, if he does not do what he teaches, is a false prophet. . . . Whoever shall say in spirit "Give me money, or something else," you shall not listen to him. But if he tells you to give on behalf of others who are in need, let none judge him. (*Didache* XI, 8, 10, 12)

The chief fruits that evidently should be looked for, then, are those of behavior (does he do what he preaches? does he behave in a Jesus-like fashion?), and generosity (any sign of greed is particularly condemned). Apparently, even for the traveling prophet to partake of a meal he has ordered "in spirit" (apparently, while supposedly in a state of trance, under the Spirit's influence and speaking on behalf of the Lord) should be taken as a sign of greediness: "And no prophet who orders a meal in spirit shall eat of it: otherwise he is a false prophet" (XI, 9). This obscure regulation suggests that the meal "ordered" by the prophet was to be distributed to others as charity. For him to take from what should have been given freely to the needy would be a sign that his concern was for himself rather than for others under the community's care. These are tough words and tougher expectations, and they have the potential, of course, to be taken too far. Indeed, there have been numerous cases of kind-hearted pastors treated poorly by their greedy congregations, and not just instances of greedy clergy. But, as a general rule, these strictures on those claiming spiritual authority are in accord with Jesus' warning: Watch out for false prophets, who are in it for what they can get, not for what they can give. Watch for the fruit. As always, Jesus is a pragmatist of the first order.

The remaining two sets of opposing images, that of the two gates and ways, and that of the two houses and their foundations, apply to more than just those aspiring to any sort of community leadership among the disciples of Jesus. These two parables apply to us all, with no distinction between callings. From these, I wish to draw attention to only the most obvious and necessary features.

In the parable of the two gates and ways, Jesus' stress is on the "narrow" and "hard" aspects of the gate and way "that leads to life," and how "few" they are "who find it." Elsewhere Jesus says that his "yoke is easy" and his "burden is light" (Matt. 11:30). There would, at first blush, appear to be a contradiction here; and yet I would argue that such is not the case. As with any serious school of spiritual discipleship, there is a decision to be made: one must choose between the discipline that leads to interior transformation and the "broad" and "easy" path of continuing on without it.

As wide and easy as that latter way seems, it is hardly one without its own numerous troubles, and, invariably, it is a life concluded by death. Without any self-knowledge and an inner change during one's existence, death rings down the curtain on a life lacking significance or meaning.

"Destruction" is the term Jesus uses, with all its rough frankness. "Repentance," we may recall, means "changing one's mind" — an inner confrontation with one's self and, in some greater way, with God. (Even if we wish to call "God" by another name, whether personal or impersonal, we can't evade the truth of a reality that transcends our selves, and which has on occasion throughout our lives had some sort of draw on us.) However, once we have opted to change, to rearrange our insides, to let God work on us, and to be disciples of Jesus and embrace his kingdom, we discover that his "yoke" and his "burden" not only do not crush us; they cause us to become fully and deeply human. We grow up, we learn to love, we learn to act and believe and live freely and meaningfully. It's "hard and narrow" to remove from ourselves those aspects of our lives that are addictive, selfish, and petty, not to mention malicious and even evil; but we are better off for it as we go on, and stick to the road, and continue to come back to Jesus whenever we stray, no matter what. And after a while most of us will have no real desire ever to go back to the wide and easy (and flat and dull and terminally stupid) way of destruction. Its appeal will gradually fade away, and we will see it as the great and wide sham it is and always was and always will prove to be.

The other image — that of the two houses — reminds us that our foundation is to be "hearing *and doing*" the words of Jesus, and not "hearing *and not doing*" them. The pragmatism of Jesus is again in evidence. The foundation of the house we are meant to be building within and among us is, finally, a matter of living the Sermon on the Mount. Either we take Jesus at his word in this instance, or we do not. But — if we take him at his word — then our "salvation" rests on whether or not we are prepared at least to attempt daily *to live* according to the teachings we have been exploring together in this book. Jesus says nothing here that is not aimed at our way of living life. He is not, it seems, overly concerned that we get every jot and tittle of our theology correct (whatever being theologically "correct" might mean among the multitude of divergent and conflicting theologies). He is *not* concerned that we comprehend some system of dogmas or abstract doctrines, or can adequately define the theory of "atonement," or can speak eloquently about "the economic Trinity," or have some precisely defined theory of his presence in the Holy Communion. All that may be quite interesting and even enlightening for those of us with theological leanings and/or credentials. But Jesus isn't concerned about any of that. He is concerned that we be humble, makers of peace, as inclusively loving as the heavenly Father, ready to care for the poor, ready to forgive all, rooting out of our selves lust and anger and other twisting passions that distort our lives and relationships, and developing a host of other practical qualities that characterize those who wish to seek first the kingdom of God and his righteousness.

The foundation is hearing and doing, and what has been heard is eminently practical. What remains is the doing; and that is the work of all our lifetimes, if we are his disciples, regardless of when we started or when we finish here on earth.

16

The Sermon That Has No End

—⟨⟨∞⟩⟩—

*28And when Jesus finished these sayings, the crowds were as-
tonished at his teaching, 29for he taught them as one who had
authority, and not as their scribes.*

The Sermon on the Mount is never an address from which we
can walk away, as if it is concluded and now we can move
along to more profound things. It is, as we have seen, the very
heart and soul and foundation of our lives as disciples of Jesus. It
stands, along with other sayings of Jesus such as his parables, as
the most fundamental groundwork of his teaching; but it can
never be transcended, either theologically or mystically or ethi-
cally. We must keep coming back to it. It remains the constant
touchstone by which we see if our faith is gold or not.

It gives us a theoretical frame for the conduct of our individual
and communal lives. It is not, however, concerned with theory as
such. Very little in the way of abstraction is in it. It lacks those
speculative and trifling elements that are typically deemed to be
serious "theology" in a learned or scholastic context. Jesus is not a
theologian, except in the most mystical sense of that word. As I
have said repeatedly throughout this book, his is a pragmatic
body of teachings.

Although it provides no hard-and-fast polity for church government or organization, Jesus' Sermon does give the principles and guidelines for the ethical pattern or method of operation of any community (Catholic, Orthodox, Anglican, Lutheran, Presbyterian, Methodist, Baptist, Mennonite, Evangelical Free, Pentecostal, non-denominational, and so on) that gathers in his name and attempts to be a witness for God's kingdom.

I can envision a community of disciples, in fact, who suspend all abstractly theoretical considerations as being central to their communal life, and endeavor instead to delve as seekers into, and absorb as best they can, the principles and guidance of Jesus' sayings. Such an experimental community would need to be small, or made up of small cells of people, who could discuss and pray and work together as if under the direct supervision of Jesus himself. The emphasis would be not on the intangible or the subtly theological, but on the concrete and pragmatic — on contemplative experience and loving action. Whatever did not serve the attempt to live daily in accord with the way of life of the kingdom of heaven and its "Torah" would be regarded as nonessential, and certainly not a cause to break fellowship or mutual encouragement. Such a Jesus-centered experiment might be precisely the sort of thing most needed today, whatever the context socially, politically, culturally, or religiously.

Likewise, the Sermon on the Mount calls us as individuals to examine our lives at their deepest levels and to work strenuously on our own, ongoing transformation. It is a handbook for disciples who wish to shape their interior lives in such a way that, no matter what the practical daily functions of a community of disciples may look like, the disciple's personal ethic and behavior remains consistent with the character of God's kingdom and righteousness. Jesus may not teach anything like an Emersonian version of self-reliance, but he does teach us to take responsibility for our individual lives before God. We are to stand on our own two feet, be the owners of our own faith, and

be Jesus' disciples before any other allegiance we may legitimately claim.

The highest expression of our imitation of Jesus, both collec-
tively and individually, is in our concrete actions of love. First, we
are to love those who, like us, are imperfect disciples gathered in
some form of communal life. Then, second, we are to exhibit our
love as a community dedicated to the kingdom of heaven outward
into the world around us. Everything Jesus teaches us has some
relation to this theme, whether it's a matter of economics and
ownership, of sexuality and married life, of humility and integrity,
of not judging and criticizing others, of peacemaking, or of good
deeds done for the poor. It all has to do with love for others, which
is the purest expression of our love of God. If Jesus has a theology,
it is a "theology of humanism" — we love God through love of the
humanity made in his image.

Lastly, as we descend from the mountain, it is important that
it be understood that what I have written here is one man's — one
very faulty man's — reflections on the Sermon of Jesus. Perhaps
these thoughts have been occasionally idiosyncratic. I think that's
to be expected, really. I suppose your own thoughts about Jesus'
Sermon are just as personal, just as to a great extent they should
be. After all, you must own your discipleship as I must own mine.

This collection of my musings on the text is hardly meant to be
the last word, not even my own last word, about it. I will return to
it again and again, as I imagine so shall you. Each time we may see
new things, feel new pangs as we are struck with the realization of
how far short we fall of the ideal set by Jesus, but we will also derive
new vigor as we continue on in our lives with Jesus. It is a Sermon
that has no end, at least not in this life. Like the seed of the kingdom itself, it grows like a living thing in us, and we grow in it.

Or, like the gate in T. S. Eliot's poem, it will always be somewhat "unknown" to us even as it is "remembered" by us over and
over again. We will need to come and pass through it often, until
finally we pass through an even greater unknown gate.

Questions for Discussion and Reflection

CHAPTER ONE

1. Why does Hart say that the question uppermost in the minds of Jesus' first listeners was "How should I live my life?" Do you think he's right? Should this be the question with which we approach the teachings of Jesus today?
2. Why does the author bring his personal history to our attention? Is it relevant? If so, what are the implications for us and for our personal stories?
3. Why does Hart say that faith is primarily personal and individual?

CHAPTER TWO

1. What does "repentance" literally mean, and how is this different from ways the word is frequently misunderstood? What might be the consequences of understanding it according to its literal meaning?
2. What does "kingdom of heaven" mean? Why was this term in-

flammatory in Jesus' time? How might it prove to be provocative today?

3. Why are the teachings of Jesus still vital today? Think about their importance for our lives, our communities, our country, and our world.

CHAPTER THREE

1. What new understandings of the Beatitudes did you get from this chapter?

2. Jesus blessed "the poor in spirit" and "peacemakers." In today's world, what challenges do these two blessings present for us if we intend to follow Jesus?

3. What are the implications for us of Hart's statement that "To live as Jesus intended means we are meant to 'drop out' in some ways"?

CHAPTER FOUR

1. In what way is Jesus' preaching of the kingdom an interpretation of the Torah? In what specific ways is Jesus' teaching a *radical* revision of it?

2. Why does Hart say, "One of the greatest disservices ever perpetrated by the church was not sufficiently dissuading many of its own defenders and theologians from declaiming so many things that never really needed to be talked about at all"? To what things does he perhaps refer? Is he too harsh?

3. What are the "invisible and visible aspects of righteousness"?

CHAPTER FIVE

1. Hart provides a very different picture of Gehenna ("hell"), as originally taught by Jesus, than traditions and later theologi-

cal systems came to present. What are these differences, and why do they (or don't they) matter?

2. Hart says that lust is the opposite of love. What does he mean by that?

3. In your opinion, has Hart made any valuable points about the subject of divorce? Are any of these points new to you?

CHAPTER SIX

1. Why does Jesus forbid the making of vows? What practical consequences might follow for us if we take this injunction to heart?

2. Jesus commands us — even when we are faced with injustice — not to seek recompense or to exact revenge. He teaches that true justice is neither proportionate nor retaliatory. What practical implications does this have for our lives?

3. How do we fulfill Jesus' saying that we must be "perfect, as your heavenly Father is perfect"?

CHAPTER SEVEN

1. Why does Jesus use the strong word "beware" when he teaches us not to perform our works of piety "before men"?

2. How and why does Jesus radicalize piety?

3. "Character is seen by action." In what ways might this be understood as a key to authentic discipleship?

CHAPTER EIGHT

1. What possible effect on the poor can public displays of charity have? How does Jesus teach us to give with appropriate consideration?

2. Why was equality among Jesus' followers considered so important by them? Should it become an ideal for us today?

3. Why does Hart say, "Jesus had a lot to say about finances, and none of it had to do with financial security or the accumulation of personal wealth"? What does this mean for our life goals and our pursuit of success, and how we should regard wealth?

CHAPTER NINE

1. Jesus stresses individual personal prayer. Why is this kind of prayer vital for our lives?

2. What should the role of contemplative prayer be in our lives? What statements about such prayer in the text stood out for you?

3. What does Jesus mean for us to understand about the Father's role in our lives as it is presented to us in the Lord's Prayer? What is the outcome in the way we perceive God?

CHAPTER TEN

1. In what ways can our fasting be related practically to the needs of the poor?

2. In what ways might we effectively practice fasting today? How might we help one another do it?

3. What could "mindful fasting" look like for us? In what sense would it be "mindful"?

CHAPTER ELEVEN

1. Why does Hart state emphatically that "Jesus was not a capitalist"? What word *would* describe Jesus' teachings on economic issues?

2. Jesus warns us against giving in to anxiety. Why? How might we discipline our thoughts not to give in to it?

3. How does Hart tie our tendencies to be anxious to the fears some have (or exploit) concerning the "end times"? What would be a proper perspective on such matters?

CHAPTER TWELVE

1. What does "judging" another mean, particularly in the light of James 4:11-12 and 1 Corinthians 4:3-5?

2. How should we deal with fellow disciples who truly need correction? How do we both judge and yet "not judge"?

3. What is the role of "detachment"? What does it mean, and how should we put it into practice? Related to this, what does Hart say is our "general rule of thumb"?

CHAPTER THIRTEEN

1. How does Hart connect Matthew 7:6 with Matthew 15:21-28? What lesson does he derive from the comparison?

2. What distinctions exist between "those inside" and "those outside" the community of Jesus' disciples?

3. What do such harsh terms as "dogs" and "swine," as used by Jesus, really mean?

CHAPTER FOURTEEN

1. What are the "good things" Jesus refers to in the Golden Rule? How might this relate to Luke's version of the same saying?

2. Why does Jesus refer to us as "evil," and what does it mean? How do we feel when he uses such tough language?

3. What does Hart mean when he refers to the teachings of Jesus as "essential pragmatism"? What is "pragmatism"? How does pragmatism relate to truth?

CHAPTER FIFTEEN

1. What does Jesus say about "false prophets"? Are there false prophets today? Why are Jesus' warnings so tough?
2. Once again, the stress is on "doing" (not just hearing) what Jesus teaches. How are we to understand the language of "judgment" in light of this heavy emphasis? What practical considerations should this engender in us?
3. How does "salvation" relate to the "practical qualities" that Jesus teaches? Can we have an authentic understanding of the first without the second? What do we mean by "salvation"?

CHAPTER SIXTEEN

1. What experimental idea does Hart propose as the basis of a community of seekers who desire to take seriously the sayings of Jesus? Is it possible?
2. In what sense are disciples of Jesus expected individually to be self-reliant? What would a community of such self-reliant, but mutually supportive, disciples look like?
3. Why does Hart say provocatively that "if Jesus has a theology" — meaning "theology" in a formal sense — "it is a 'theology of humanism'"? Why do you suppose he uses intentionally controversial language? What is he trying to stir up by using it?

Talking Sense about the Words of Jesus

———⟨⟨⟨⟨⟩⟩⟩⟩———

I want to present here what I believe is a sensible approach to the sayings of Jesus.

First, what do I *not* mean by "the sayings of Jesus"? Assuming we want to know what *Jesus himself* said, what should we exclude from serious consideration? Following are four suggestions.

We should exclude some of the more evidently dubious ways that Jesus' sayings have been used down through the ages, no matter how venerable the "users."

Churches have often made questionable use of the Gospel sayings of Jesus to justify theological systems and dogmatic formulae, temporal authority and political ends, canon law, and so forth. One can discover numerous instances of this down through the centuries. It is the nature of institutions and nations to bolster their influence with expedient defenses in whatever context they find themselves. The church has often backed its own claims of authority with carefully selected, but doubtfully interpreted, sayings of Jesus. Not every historically or doctrinally useful interpretation of Jesus' sayings concocted behind ecclesiastical chamber doors should be accepted as forever ironclad and true to him, even if that church — whichever church that might be — has plausible reason to claim to be "the pillar and bulwark of the truth" (1 Tim. 3:15). Indeed, in making such a claim, the church — any church claiming allegiance to Christ, that is — should be especially conscientious about getting the Lord's words right, even if that means revising from time to time some previous interpretation when it can be shown to have been mistaken. The church, of all institutions, should be the most open to conforming itself to what Jesus *actually meant,* and, if it doesn't know what this or that saying in context actually meant, it should refrain from pretending it does.

What is, however, to the church's everlasting credit is that it has preserved for us the Four Gospels, which give us the best insights into the meaning of Jesus, even when some of his sayings have not always fit comfortably with later dogmas about him. (For instance, there is his claim in Mark 13:32 of *limitations to his knowledge,* or his seeming *change of mind* — in the best manuscripts of John 7:8-10 — both of which could be unsettling for some with strict dogmatic presuppositions.) When, therefore, we refer to Jesus' sayings, we mean above all the sayings in the Four Gospels (and the two minor canonical sayings outside them — Acts 20:35 and 1 Corinthians 9:14), as they stand and according to their most likely meaning within their own context.

We should treat with caution non-canonical sayings of Jesus, including them in our considerations only insofar as they aid understanding of the canonical words.

Let's take the most popular of these texts as an example. *The Gospel of Thomas* is a fascinating work, comprised entirely of sayings. Scholars have had good reason to study this apocryphal gospel in particular, since many of its sayings echo those found in Matthew and Luke. However, in the case of *Thomas,* we unfortunately have only a third- or fourth-century Coptic translation of a non-extant, second-century Greek text (recovered at Nag Hammadi in Egypt in 1947). In other words, we don't have the original version, and what we do have has so many "Gnosticizing" elements in it that we can't always be sure how much is genuine and how much has been altered. Whatever there is in it that comes from Jesus himself has been worked over to fit a "Gnostic" system of a later period. There is good reason to think that *Thomas* contains some genuine, relatively "pure" sayings of Jesus, but we need to be very cautious with such a text. This caveat applies to all the other, even less credible early texts containing what purport to be the teachings of Christ.

We should exclude the "Sayings Gospel of Q" — which doesn't rightly exist, despite laudable scholarly efforts to "reconstruct" it.

I have found these efforts interesting and indeed plausible in many instances. I lean on such scholarship for enlightenment regarding the cultural context and likely meaning of this or that saying. Still, we don't have any actual document that is "Q." ("Q" is a cipher which derives from the German word for "source" — *Quelle* — and refers in scholarly circles to a *non-extant* and therefore *hypothetical* compilation from which both Matthew and Luke supposedly drew when composing their Gospels.) So, we need once again to exercise caution.

Was there ever a "disciples' handbook" of sayings, as some think Q may have been? It seems quite likely, but we don't possess it — at least not yet. (But who knows if someday another great discovery will be made and there will be found some text along the lines of what we now think of as Q?) Was Q, if it existed at all, in fact a "sayings" collection, as is *Thomas?* Well, possibly; but perhaps there never was such a gospel, and Matthew and Luke took their mutual "Jesus sayings" from a gospel that was — like Mark — a *narrative* gospel, one that included Jesus' miracles, death, and resurrection (and which also might help explain the many narrative differences between the Synoptics). Perhaps Mark itself was an *abridgement* of a longer narrative work that *did* include all or many of the sayings we now attribute to Q. Perhaps. We simply don't know. And it's the simple, obvious fact of *not knowing* which makes it tenuous to base any *conclusions* about Jesus' authentic sayings on a hypothetical Q.

We should exclude all later "private revelations" given to saints and mystics, said to derive from Jesus.

I include this mainly for those who come from traditions that have permitted the elevation of such things to a level quite nearly equaling the Gospel sayings themselves. It should not need to be said, really, but say it I shall: No "locutions" said to come from Jesus (or Mary, for that matter) are to be taken as authoritative for knowing what it means to follow Jesus. Many of them express fine sentiments, and no one should think that anyone claiming to have had such an experience has found nothing valuable spiritually *for them* in it. But there it ends. No one else need feel in any way answerable to such "sayings" alleged to have come from heaven, let alone troubled or guilty about simply ignoring them. Indeed, if the claimed "locution" includes an insistence that the message go out to others publicly, this should be all the justification one needs to run from it. In this matter, one should heed the wisdom of the likes of the Desert Fathers and St. John of the Cross, who held dim views of such things and saw in them far more in the way of temptation than of blessing.

It is enough to listen to the sayings and narratives we possess in the canon. These things are demanding enough, and their meaning unfolds for us over a lifetime of meditation. We need not clutter our heads with other, vastly inferior sayings said to come from on high, most of which sound nothing like anything the authentic Christ actually said or would have been inclined to say (and if they don't sound like him, then we are right to doubt they have come from him). This is not to disparage the idea of, say, prophecy — as long as the "prophet" has something truly practical to say, possesses evident humility, and doesn't act as if he or she is Jesus' special friend.

Now I turn to the sayings of Jesus we should know and trust, and how we can approach them intelligently. I refer to the sayings as we find them, in all their various forms, within the Four Gospels of the New Testament canon. These Gospels give us those portraits, those "icons," of Jesus which the great majority of early Christians embraced as most true to him. This claim has been debated in recent years, of course, but the evidence nevertheless supports the older, less fashionable conclusion. They are narratives, and the emphasis of each is the passion, death, and resurrection of Christ. Without the contours of this great story, told with significant variations by our canonical four versions, we would not have the context for the sayings by which we live.

In fact, the sayings of Jesus become strikingly powerful for us because of the story that frames them. We are moved by the person of Jesus, by his character of compassion, his intensity of purpose, his strength, and — if we are able to pick up on the Greek text, for instance, of Mark — even his rough masculine qualities. If we are paying attention, we cannot help but be surprised by his inclusion of women among his disciples (simply not done in his culture!), his elevation of the status of children (shocking disregard for propriety!), his denunciations of religious hypocrisy (so much a feature of his teachings in all four Gospels that one cannot dismiss them as merely the additions of a later generation, no matter how they may have been honed by the evangelists of a subsequent age to suit their own apologetic ends), and so forth.

The passion narratives constitute the central motif of Christian salvation. In their drama we are all included as witnesses, we are invited into a covenant through sacrifice, we see redemption (liberation) at work through suffering and horrific judicial murder, and we see God's vindication of his Son through the Resurrection. In Mark, we have this narrative presented as the grim incentive to follow Christ at all costs, even unto death; in Matthew, we have it as the beginning of the general resurrection and vindication of the saints, and the call to baptize and teach all nations; in Luke, it is the proof of the Kingdom's coming, supplemented by Christ's ascension, session, and sending of the Holy Spirit; and, in John, it is the restoration of Paradise, the healing of "the sin of the world," the realization of new birth from above.

The narratives themselves vary, although Matthew, Mark, and Luke (the "Synoptic" — the "Seeing Together" — Gospels) follow for the most part the same sequence of events. John departs significantly, detailing a Judean ministry not mentioned in the Synoptic Gospels, which, in comparison, focus on a Galilean ministry before his final journey to Jerusalem. The Synoptics give the impression of a ministry lasting about a year, while John suggests one at least three years long. Even when John describes an incident in Jesus' life that is likewise found in the other three Gospels — such as the interaction between Jesus and John the Baptist, the cleansing of the Temple (which he places at the outset of Jesus' ministry, while the Synoptics put it in the final week of his life), the feeding of the five thousand, and more — it is given a distinct meaning in the narrative.

Furthermore, even the Synoptics differ among themselves, adding and subtracting this or that, and making their chronologies fit their particular interpretations of the message they strive to convey. The fathers of the church were not blind to these distinctions, but saw in them no insurmountable difficulties. In other words, they were not, for the most part, what we would consider to be literalists. In the special case of John, the fathers maintained from the earliest centuries that this was a "spiritual" Gospel — apparently meaning that it was clearly not to be read as literally as the other three, and that the interpretations of the incidents recounted there and the lengthy monologues put on the lips of Jesus (or, it might be argued, the "fleshing out" of shorter, pithier, possibly arcane, but authentic statements of his — a point I will come back to below) were "revelations" of the Spirit regarding the meaning of his coming (an aspect perhaps hinted at in John 14:26; see also 1 John 2:20, 27).

Each of these Gospels also gives us a different Christology from the others; but these differences, placed side by side in the New Testament canon, converged and crisscrossed within the overall tradition as a result. Harmonizations of the Four Gospels into single, doctored narratives appear to have been produced by Tatian, circa A.D. 150. An Assyrian who studied under Justin Martyr, he produced his *Diatessaron,* which survives, sometime during this period. Such efforts reveal how soon after the apostolic generation these four texts, already taken as authoritative, were being reworked and reshaped to create a unified portrait of Christ. It is also significant that these four were given such prestige, and not any of the other, later, and considerably less reliable gospels. Still, harmonizations inevitably falsify the revealing distinctiveness of each individual Gospel's perspective; and — wisely — the fathers of the church ultimately included in the canon the Four Gospels in their integrity, and not a single mishmash of them all.

It should not surprise us that this most mysterious of men was interpreted in various ways, even by those closest to him. Biographers are by necessity themselves always *interpreters* of their subjects, mainly because every human life contains vast complexities, nuances, and imponderables. How much more is this the case with Jesus, who neatly fitted none of the categories of his day, not to mention our own — indeed, who seemed quite often to contradict the very categories either he or his followers assigned to him? How to define one whose demeanor and sensational deeds transcended the normal, but whose humility and lowliness and charity reached to the most neglected and base of his society? How to understand both his lordliness of behavior and his slavish execution? How to reconcile his amazing miracles of healing with his ignominious crucifixion at the hands of the Romans, and with the collusion of the religious establishment of his own people? How to comprehend that he was encountered alive by his disciples after his monstrous death? No easy task for those who sought to communicate who and what Jesus was to later generations of the movement he had begun, especially as that movement spread from the backwaters of Palestine into the rest of the Roman Empire and among the Gentiles. Each Gospel provides a different support for what would undergird the church's final completed structure of Christology. All four, in one way or another, give us both a "divine" and a "human" Jesus, if we mean by these terms something less precise than what would emerge creedally in the Greek and Latin church after centuries of debate.

Although the church necessarily focused on the question of *who* Jesus was and *from whence* came his authority, a *personal* authority that claimed to override both the traditions of his people's religious establishment and the power of the world's greatest empire, that very authority was articulated first and foremost through his teachings. That is to say, his message of God's kingdom was a message about how to live one's life rightly before God. It was neither a "conservative" nor a "liberal" message, but it was a *radical* body of teachings. It struck at the roots of human behavior and revealed "the way" of life. The sayings of Jesus challenge all aspects of and glib notions about what it means to live in this world; they disrupt and overturn complacency, the status quo, our "I'm only human" excuses, and the inclination to put anything before God and neighbor. They are uncompromising and demand commitment and self-discipline. In these sayings we find the *substance* of Jesus' authority (which Christological definitions and creeds exist only to serve), and therefore this *substance* should be the most vital center of attention in our lives. Pietists of all ages have been right in their assertion that we really are meant *to live now in this world intentionally* according to, say, the terms laid down in the Sermon on the Mount.

So, before going one step further, I will say outright that Jesus' teachings, as we have received them, and with only a handful of notable qualifications, are *perennial* and *pragmatic.* They are perennial because they are applicable to human existence in every place and time. Sayings about love of God and man, forgiveness of others, nonviolent resistance, avoiding religious hypocrisy, giving, self-denial, simplicity, prayer, refusal to judge others, reliance on a universally loving "Father in heaven" (whom we may call *Abba*), and more — these sayings are timeless.

Likewise, they are pragmatic, in that nothing Jesus taught was meant to be left in the realm of abstractions and doctrinal formulae. Far from it: he taught a way of life so radically opposed to the worldly way of thinking about social order in the "kingdom" (*basileia* = "empire") of Rome and elsewhere that he called it the kingdom (empire) of God. It was truly a philosophy of how to live peacefully, lovingly, philanthropically (in the truest, most self-giving sense), and in relationship to God — the path of true wisdom. We still receive his teachings as such, applying them in every age afresh, if we seek first to be his disciples.

Perennial and pragmatic, these teachings are more than institutional rubrics or a new body of legislation or a system of theology. Discipleship to Jesus, not church membership, is what the teachings of Jesus primarily entail. The latter affirms and promotes the former, or else it is empty of purpose.

So we have Matthew, Mark, Luke, and John. When we approach these four vital, seminal, and indispensable texts, we should do so with four "literary qualifications" in mind, if we intend an open and reasonable reading of them. Following are the four qualifications I suggest.

The first qualification is the matter of language.

If Jesus knew Greek at all, which was the Empire-wide *lingua franca* of his day (and there's a good chance he did, at least on a rudimentary level, because tradesmen such as he would have had to do occasional business with Gentiles living in Galilee), it is highly doubtful that he ever used it to teach during the time of his ministry. Jesus spoke Aramaic — which is why, for instance, Mark's Gospel translates his Aramaic on three occasions (5:41; 14:36; 15:34). This means that all the sayings of Jesus in the New Testament are at least one step away from the original words of Christ. And, further, when we read the Gospels in any translation and not directly in Greek, we are *two* steps away from the Aramaic Jesus actually spoke. And, in the case of John, as we will see, the possibly authentic words of Christ are a greater number of steps away from the original.

The second qualification is that of time and place.

Jesus spoke to the people of his day, and he spoke as a Jew. He addressed specifically Jewish concerns in ancient Galilee and Judea within the larger context of the Roman Empire. That is to say, we modern readers should become as acquainted with the culture and concerns of his age as we can before we presume to say what his sayings might mean for us today.

Further, we need to be aware of the fact that the immediate Palestinian culture which Jesus addressed was not identical with the cultural contexts of other regions of the empire (for example, Antioch and Rome) in which the Gospels were written decades later. The Evangelists had the task of "translating" Jesus to their own surroundings, and that sort of message-based task has always demanded adaptation. One must assume that they sought to preserve faithfully the original words and their meaning, but that they did so in ways that audiences different from the one Jesus had addressed could "get it." So, we in turn get Jesus filtered and reconfigured through the contexts of those for whom the Evangelists wrote; the earliest Gospel (Mark, it seems) was probably written a little more than four decades after the events described.

Much had occurred in those forty years, and what had occurred was nothing less than traumatic for both the people of the land Jesus had known and also for his followers of the generation once removed and abiding elsewhere. After the destruction of Jerusalem under Titus in A.D. 71, much of the world of Jesus' day was already gone forever. All four Gospels were likely set down after this shattering event, and we can be sure that its impact influenced the way the Evangelists recounted the message and life of Christ. In addition, in the decade immediately preceding the smashing of the holy city, the first great, utterly horrifying persecution of Christians, under Nero, had altered all aspects of their very existence in Rome — the most important city, next to Jerusalem, for the earliest Christians. Paul and Peter were already dead, killed before the end of the sixties, as were many of the apostolic generation. Much of the New Testament was written under the shadow of that misery, and under the shadow of the next wave of persecution, which came in the nineties under the emperor Domitian.

So, when we try to apply Jesus' evangelical words to our own culture, we must exercise some caution. By the time the Gospels were composed, Christians had already been through a great deal, with still more troubles to come; and we can be sure that these things were fresh in the Evangelists' respective minds. Most of Jesus' teaching is clearly of perennial importance, but some of it can be appreciated only if we understand the vast differences between his age and the age that immediately followed it, and then between the world(s) of the first century and the quite dissimilar one we live in.

The third qualification is that there are sometimes sayings which appear in different forms in the Gospels and reveal the editorial interpretations of the respective Evangelists.

This simple fact takes us a few more steps away from the original, since translation is mixed with obvious additional interpretation. A single example will suffice. Let's read and compare the following saying as presented in each of the first three Gospels, noting how both the immediate narrative frame and the wording vary from Gospel to Gospel:

> . . . They had only one loaf with them *in the boat.* And *he cautioned* [*the disciples*], saying, "Take heed, beware of *the leaven of the Pharisees and the leaven of Herod.*" (Mark 8:14b-15)

> *When the disciples reached the other side,* they had forgotten to bring any bread. *Jesus said to them,* "Take heed and beware of *the leaven of the Pharisees and Sadducees.*" (Matt. 16:5-6)

> In the meantime, *when so many thousands of the multitude had gathered together that they trod upon one another,* he began *to say to the disciples first,* "Beware of *the leaven of the Pharisees, which is hypocrisy.*" (Luke 12:1)

I have italicized what differs significantly in these three versions. Mark places Jesus with the disciples in a boat, and the metaphorical "leaven" he warns of is that of the Pharisees and also that of Herod. In Matthew, the disciples are onshore and out of the boat, and Jesus warns them against not only the leaven of the Pharisees, but also of the Sadducees. (Herod gets no mention.) Lastly, in Luke, there is no boat, Jesus is surrounded by multitudes he is teaching, and he speaks his warning to the disciples first, and also to others within earshot. The leaven, as in the other two Gospels, is that of the Pharisees, but this time they alone are specified, and an interpretation of what is meant by "leaven" — hypocrisy — is appended.

This is but one example among many in which we can see the Evangelists shaping their material to tell the story effectively. The saying here is probably based on actual words of Jesus preserved in the sources used for all three Gospels, and possibly it was something along the lines simply of "Beware of the leaven of the Pharisees." Where it was actually spoken — in a boat, just out of a boat, when Jesus was surrounded by a multitude, or alone with his disciples, or speaking aloud in the hearing of many, or somewhere else entirely — we don't know. We have three versions, and each one is different, and so we rightly may suspect that each Evangelist imagined the context differently. We simply accept these differences, ponder the various possible interpretations, and move on from there. We can acknowledge in what particulars they differ, and yet consider these differences not as problems so much as interesting variations on a theme. And, for heaven's sake, why not?

The fourth qualification is that of Jesus' sayings in John and how they differ from those in the Synoptic Gospels.

Many unconvincing explanations have been posited about how to reconcile John with the other Gospels. His Jesus speaks in an idiom distinct from that of the rest, using no story-parables (a hallmark of Jesus' teaching in the Synoptics); and he's given to long, rambling monologues that frequently melt or merge into the interpretive words of the Evangelist himself — which makes "red letter" editions of this Gospel and the use of quotation marks in modern texts worthless.

What we have in John, as some of the fathers were quick to explain, is a "spiritual" Gospel. What exactly that means in detail is rather slippery, admittedly, but it does indicate that early Christians saw in this highly edited text a valid revelation of the meaning of Christ. John's Gospel has sharp historical perspicacity. (John's knowledge of Jerusalem as it was in Jesus' day, before the devastation of A.D. 71, is remarkably accurate — as modern archaeology has demonstrated. He likewise shows a deft psychological insight into the various persons in the Gospels — the disciples, Nicodemus, the Samaritan woman, the cured lame man, the healed blind man, the two sisters in Bethany, Caiaphas, Pilate, and — of course — Jesus.) This Gospel also has profound mystical and allegorical elements that have proved powerful down through the ages. One might not think that such elements — prosaic and poetic, historical and mythological — could hold together well, but John manages this combination with disconcerting and inspired ease. His message is cosmic in its scope, and to appreciate what he's doing theologically, one needs to be conversant especially with the first three chapters of Genesis — his Jesus has come to restore and mend what was lost, and to bring us back with him to the Garden and the Tree of (Eternal) Life.

A number of the sayings of Jesus in this Gospel echo sayings that appear in the Synoptics. For example, the long prayer of John 17 has throughout resonances of the Lord's Prayer, which we find in two versions in Matthew and Luke (Matt. 6:9-13; Luke 11:2-4). Perhaps there is one saying in particular, which shows up in both Matthew and Luke (and thus is a "Q" — or "common source" — saying, since it is absent from Mark), that suggests that indeed Jesus did on occasion say things that sound surprisingly Johannine. It is this: "All things have been delivered to me by my Father; and no one knows the Son except the Father, and no one knows the Father except the Son and any one to whom the Son chooses to reveal him" (Matt. 11:27; the version in Luke 10:22 is almost identical). Compare this with, say, John 10:14-15b: "I am the good shepherd; I know my own and my own know me, as the Father knows me and I know the Father...." Or, again, with John 17:25: "O righteous Father, the world has not known thee, but I have known thee; and these know thee that thou hast sent me." It isn't all that difficult to believe that John's "sayings of Jesus" — those grand discourses — build on shorter, enigmatic statements Jesus made about his self-understanding. Perhaps much that Jesus says in John truly came from him in seed form — sayings such as that of Matthew 11:27 and Luke 10:22, but also such assertions as "I am the good shepherd" and more. How else to explain the early acceptance of this Gospel alongside the very dissimilar Synoptics? John's "spiritual" Gospel may be an elaboration and a deepening of shorter, authentic statements of Jesus, as early Christians possibly were affirming when they accepted this strikingly unique text into the canon.

Nevertheless, we cannot read the John sayings as we read the sayings of Jesus in the Synoptics. In his case, the words of Jesus may be three or four steps away from the original, and maybe only a bare kernel is all we might carefully regard as authentic in any given monologue. Fine. John gives us a broad and deep mystical Gospel that we can read to our immense benefit. His work is an expansive reflection, theologically rich, of Christ's meaning for the world.

So, allowing for these literary qualifications, it is our privilege to turn again and again to Jesus' own sayings for practical guidance and personal transformation above all else.

It may surprise some to hear it, but Jesus' standards are not as intolerably high as some have led us to believe. His yoke really is easy and his burden light.

For example, if we know that "love" in the Sermon on the Mount and throughout the New Testament means, as it does, *not a feeling,* but *doing good,* we can learn to love our enemies and do good to those who seek to harm us, even if we don't *feel* like it. We can turn the other cheek, give with no expectation of repayment, go the extra mile, and so forth.

Likewise, if we know that to "forgive" others refers not to some effort to readjust our *feelings,* but rather to an invitation to engage in an *action* of *non-action* — that is, a determined action of *not taking revenge* and *not doing harm* and *just dropping the matter* — then we can in fact learn to forgive, even if our anger or resentment still lingers in our feelings. Feelings determine nothing; we determine to control them.

If we understand that "not lusting" is not to be understood as "not having sexual feelings," then we realize that Jesus' exhortation is not nature-denying, but instead an insistence that we never use another as if that other were a non-person whose body and soul we imagine to exist for our pleasure. That other belongs to God, and only a respectful, self-giving mutual commitment between a man and a woman makes for the firm foundation of a truly healthy sexual union. And the list could go on.

The conclusion is this: We must take very seriously indeed that we are committed to the sayings of Jesus, to the way of life he taught, and to the practice of those sayings in our own lives individually. Before we pronounce on biblical "inerrancy," ecclesiastical tradition or authority, before even theology and devotion and liturgy, we are bound to the sayings of Jesus. This is where our personal discipleship to the one we call "Lord" brings us.

The Role of Judgment in Matthew's Gospel

O nly in Matthew's Gospel do we find Jesus identified with Isaiah's prophecy of the coming one who will be called "Emmanuel," "God with us" (Isa. 7:14; Matt. 1:23). Although Isaiah's prophecy had originally dealt with political events of his own day, this particular text came to mean for Christian readers that the long-awaited Messiah — Jesus — had come from the royal House of David, and through him God had been present in a way hitherto unknown in the history of his covenant people. Jesus Christ was not merely "the Son of David"; he was "God with us."

Matthew wanted his readers to grasp that in "Emmanuel" something has occurred that is so astounding and so new that those who profess Christ are to be judged in the light shed by this stunning revelation. Because Jesus is "God with us," how one responds to him becomes crucial and, ultimately, eternally important. Judgment is therefore already an implicit fact for one who encounters the meaning of Christ.

Judgment is therefore both *implicit* and *explicit*. In the story of the betrayal, trial, and death of Jesus, Matthew shows the *implicit* judgment at work in three different individuals' encounters with Jesus. He directs essentially the same pointed statement to each of the three, which puts all of them in the situation of pronouncing judgment upon themselves, although they fail to realize what's happening. In all three instances, Christ is seen to be the true Judge, hidden though this fact is beneath his weakness and suffering.

The first of the three encounters is that of Jesus with Judas at the Last Supper. Immediately before the institution of the Eucharist, Jesus foretells that one of the twelve disciples will betray him. The disciples, understandably shaken by this, ask one after another, "Is it I?" When it's his turn, Judas asks the question, and the Lord responds: "You have said so" (26:20-25). The second encounter is that of Jesus with the high priest, Caiaphas (26:57-66). Exasperated by Jesus' silence before the Sanhedrin, Caiaphas demands of him, "I adjure you by the living God, tell us if you are the Christ, the Son of God." Jesus' reply is identical to the one he gave earlier to Judas: "You have said so." He continues with a reference to a coming explicit judgment, however: "But I tell you, hereafter you will see the Son of Man seated at the right hand of Power, and coming on the clouds of heaven" (26:63-64). In other words, one day the tables will be turned, and Caiaphas will find himself before the true Judge — the very One he now presumes to judge. The last of the three encounters is that of Jesus with Pilate. "Are you the King of the Jews?" Pilate asks. Jesus answers (in Greek, in a slightly different form, but meaning precisely the same thing as his previous two responses): "You have said so" (27:11). Each encounter recalls the reader to something Jesus had said earlier in the Gospel: "I tell you, on the day of judgment men will render account for every careless word they utter; for by your words you will be justified, and by your words you will be condemned" (12:36-37). When Jesus says, "You have said so," he is saying, in effect, "What you have said may very well condemn you on the day of judgment."

The two interrelated instances of *explicit* judgment in Matthew are connected to a theme that runs throughout the course of his Gospel and is demonstrated by two particularly severe and sobering prophetic signs. *It is the highly significant theme of the judgment of corrupt or falsified religion.* If in Jesus "God is with us," we might well expect that that religion born of supernatural revelation to the patriarchs and prophets before his coming would itself undergo a test — a crisis — when he showed up and took stock of it. The Old Testament seers had warned of divine visitation from time to time, in general terms, and of its possible consequences. With the coming of Christ, the religion of the Temple and synagogue found itself literally face-to-face with its Messianic redeemer, and, as Matthew and other Gospels tell it, the great difference between the two — the religion and the Lord — rapidly became a scene of open conflict.

Turning first to the *second* prophetic action of the two, we find that it involves — of all things — the cursing of a *fruitless* fig tree (21:18-22). In order to understand this odd action, we must recall three earlier statements in the Gospel likening false religion to a tree that bears bad fruit. These three statements will help us understand the meaning of the cursing of the tree.

The first statement is made when Matthew introduces us to John the Baptist. When "many of the Pharisees and Sadducees" come to be baptized by him(!), he ferociously denounces them:

> "You brood of vipers! Who warned you to flee from the wrath to come? Bear fruit that befits repentance, and do not presume to say to yourselves, 'We have Abraham as our father'; for I tell you, God is able from these stones to raise up children to Abraham. Even now the axe is laid to the root of the trees; every tree therefore that does not bear good fruit is cut down and thrown into the fire." (3:7-10)

The second statement is found near the conclusion of the Sermon on the Mount. Jesus is speaking about "false prophets, who come to you in sheep's clothing but inwardly are ravenous wolves" (7:15), and warns of false religion:

"You will know them by their fruits. Are grapes gathered from thorns, or figs from thistles? So, every sound tree bears good fruit, but the bad tree bears evil fruit. A sound tree cannot bear evil fruit, nor can a bad tree bear good fruit. Every tree that does not bear good fruit is cut down and thrown into the fire. Thus you will know them by their fruits." (7:16-20)

The third statement occurs during one of the most heated conflicts between Jesus and the Pharisees. They accuse him of casting out demons, not by the Holy Spirit, but "by Beelzebul, the prince of demons" (12:24). Jesus makes it clear to them that such an accusation is, at least potentially, a blasphemy against the Holy Spirit. He continues with these words: "Either make the tree good, and its fruit good; or make the tree bad, and its fruit bad; for the tree is known by its fruit. You brood of vipers!" (33-34a).

These three earlier statements not only set us up for the story of the hapless fig tree, but also for the other and earlier of the *explicit* signs of judgment — that of Jesus' "cleansing" the Temple (21:12-13). With this prophetic action, Jesus proclaims, "It is written, 'My house shall be called a house of prayer'; but you make it a den of robbers." Both actions — the cleansing of the Temple and the cursing of the fig tree — reinforce one another, indeed mean the same thing: together they constitute a clear manifestation of God's judgment on the religion of the Temple.

After the Temple cleansing, the chief priests and scribes are indignant at how Jesus is being received by the children, who are crying, "Hosanna to the Son of David!" (vv. 14-17, a passage most profitably read with 18:1-6 and 19:13-15 in mind). These supposed custodians of God's Law are likewise incensed about "the wonderful things that [Jesus] did." Verse 14 tells precisely what these wonderful things were: "And the blind and the lame came to him in the Temple, and he healed them." This verse, found only in Matthew, is also a subtle prophetic sign. He who is now being hailed by his followers as "Son of David" now outdoes David himself, showing himself merciful where David most emphatically was not. This verse contrasts sharply with the words found in the Septuagint's rendering of an incident in David's career, recounted in 2 Samuel 5:8: "Therefore it is said, 'The blind and the lame shall not come into the House of the Lord'" — words that are directly related to David's "hatred of soul" for the blind and the lame, which he expressed during his conquering of Jerusalem a millennium before Christ's appearing. Jesus reveals his grace and power to the blind, the lame, and the children — those who represent "the least of these my brethren" (25:40). "Great David's greater Son" thus outshines David. The religious authorities despise him for it.

Then comes, as I said, the fig tree incident (21:18-22), another sign of decisive judgment given to the disciples:

> In the morning, as he was returning to the city, he was hungry. And seeing *one fig tree* by the wayside he went to it, and found nothing on it but leaves only. And he said to it, "May no fruit ever come from you again!" And the fig tree withered at once. When the disciples saw it they marveled, saying, "How did the fig tree wither at once?" And Jesus answered them, "Truly, I say to you, if you have faith and never doubt, you will not only do what has been done to the fig tree, but even if you say to this mountain, 'Be taken up and cast into the sea,' it will be done. And whatever you ask in prayer, you will receive, if you have faith." [The italicized words are translated directly from the Greek.]

In Greek, the fig tree is clearly designated by Matthew as "*one* fig tree." (It is unfortunate that translations invariably render this "a fig tree.") This is significant, because Matthew is often given to *doubling* in his Gospel accounts of events: *two* demoniacs in 8:28-34, not one as in Mark and Luke; *two* blind men each in both 9:27-31 and 20:29-34; and *two* donkeys for Jesus to ride in 21:1-7. (This literary device may signify the inclusion of both Jew and Gentile in the kingdom, but this is only a conjecture; see Eph. 2:11-22.) It seems noteworthy, then, that he appears to emphasize that there was only "*one* fig tree."

The fact that Jesus responds to his disciples' astonished query about this strange deed with a teaching on *prayer* picks up on what he had decried only a few short verses earlier as notably lacking in the Temple: "It is written, 'My house shall be called a house of prayer'; but you make it a den of robbers." The fig tree is *fruitless* — as are the Temple and the religion Jesus confronts there. "One" fig tree is judged with a dreadful malediction for its fruitlessness; one form of revealed religion will similarly meet with judgment for its own barrenness: "Behold, your house is forsaken and desolate. For I tell you, you will not see me again, until you say, 'Blessed is he who comes in the name of the Lord'" (23:38-39). And — recall — the One who there and then forsakes the Temple is "God with us." In the place of this forsaken and desolate "house of prayer," the Lord begins to build his disciples into a new house of prayer: "Whatever you ask in prayer, you will receive, if you have faith." Or, to shift to the other metaphor at work here, in place of "one" barren fig tree, Christ plants another, which, through faith, is intended to bear fruit. (That there is indeed *another* — that is, a *second* — "fig tree" may be inferred from 24:32-33.)

The image of the fruitless fig tree is also complemented by the parable of the evil vinedressers in 21:33-46, where the Lord's desire for a "fruit-bearing nation" is stressed as the reason for God's new action in Christ: "Therefore I say to you, the Kingdom of God will be taken from you and given to a nation bearing the fruits of it" (21:43).

If any ambiguity regarding the nature of the sign of the fig tree and the judgment it portended lingered in the disciples' minds afterward, it must have been dispelled when Jesus said, in response to their excited wonder before the magnificent buildings of the Temple, "You see all these, do you not? Truly, I say to you, there will not be left here one stone upon another, that will not be thrown down" (24:2). And the judgment he pronounced may be seen to begin at the very moment of Jesus' death on the cross: "And behold, the curtain of the Temple was torn in two, from top to bottom" (27:51).

The fig tree stands as a sign of judgment on corrupt, barren, falsified religion. But perhaps the sharpest edge of the point Jesus is making, especially from the later perspective of Matthew's readers, is no longer directed at the old form of religion, *but now directed at the adherents of the new.* There is an implicit — *pragmatic* — warning for Christ's church in it which should not be overlooked. For Jesus' followers to avoid a similar judgment on fruitless and hypocritical religion, they must take careful heed of the examples of the Pharisees and Sadducees (cf. 16:6).

It is the very nature of judgment that by it two inherently irreconcilable things, hitherto mingled, are finally separated. Two ultimate possibilities reach their appointed and necessary divergence. "Enter by the narrow gate; for the gate is wide and the way is easy, that leads to destruction, and those who enter by it are many. For the gate is narrow and the way is hard, that leads to life, and those who find it are few" (7:13-14). Repeatedly the Lord reminds his disciples through his parables that there will be a separation, a judgment, and that it will in fact begin, in the words of 1 Peter 4:17, in the household of God. On that day those who have heard the initial invitation to enter the kingdom of heaven will be divided. "Not every one who says to me, 'Lord, Lord,' shall enter the kingdom of heaven, but he who does the will of my Father who is in heaven" (Matt. 7:21). The final division will be determined by whether or not one has built one's life pragmatically on "rock" or foolishly on "sand." In other words, whether or not one has both heard and done (not just heard) "these words of mine" (7:24-27).

So it is that the parables realistically present the kingdom as it appears externally in this age as a mixed bag. It contains wheat and tares (13:24-30, 36-43), good and bad fish (13:47-50), obedient and wicked servants (24:45-51), wise and foolish virgins (25:1-13), and productive and slothful stewards of their Master's property (25:14-30). All these are destined for separation when the Day of Judgment comes. Indeed, the culminating parable of Matthew, the one to which all the others lead up, is that of the Great Judgment in 25:31-46, wherein the two categories to be evaluated and separated forever are likened to sheep and goats.

The parables depict a future division into two groups of persons, one under benediction and the other under malediction, among those who share something of the kingdom's reality here and now. That both good and bad are, before the end of the age, found within the precincts of the kingdom is a reminder that God's generosity is comprehensive, and that God's reign extends throughout the cosmos and encompasses all. Thus the disciples are pointedly told to emulate their heavenly Father, who universally and indiscriminately "makes his sun rise on the evil and on the good, and sends rain on the just and on the unjust" (5:43-48). Jesus, "God with us," embodies this same non-prejudicial bestowal of divine favor during his ministry: The Pharisees asked Jesus' disciples, "Why does your teacher eat with tax collectors and sinners?" (9:11). Yet, although God includes all sorts in his kingdom now, the Great Judgment must inevitably divide the bad from the good before there can be a perfected creation.

The parable of 25:31-46 is the ultimate parabolic icon of this theme in Matthew's Gospel, concluding the final series of parables in chapters 24 and 25. This last grouping of parables deals specifically with the conduct of Christ's disciples as they live in preparation for his return. That is, the logic of the whole sequence leads to the inference that this parable — like those that immediately precede it — is about *the judgment of those who profess Christ.* The One on the throne is the Son of Man, a title that corresponds to the name "Emmanuel." Before him are "gathered all the nations." What the Son of Man will do is "separate them one from another as a shepherd separates the sheep from the goats." By the term "nations" *(ethne)* we are meant to understand *all those who come to believe in the gospel* and are gathered from "all nations" — those to whom the disciples are sent to preach after the Resurrection (28:19), and who answer the call to follow Jesus and are baptized "in the name of the Father and of the Son and of the Holy Spirit." But at the Judgment, all who have been brought together from the "nations" — wheat and tares, good and bad fish, obedient and wicked servants, wise and foolish virgins, and productive and lazy stewards — are to be divided one from another. *They will be separated on the basis of what, ultimately, constitutes the line of difference between good and bad religion.* And that line is itself drawn by the Son of Man, who here spells out definitively what it means to embrace the truth that "God is with us" — that God is in our very midst, visible in his image and likeness, discernable in the faces of human beings.

Once again, what should be noted emphatically here — and what has frequently been overlooked by exegetes — is that Matthew is *not at all* presenting here a picture of the judgment of *un*believers. Nothing in the immediate context could lead us to the evasive conclusion that the judgment upon the "goats" is a judgment upon those outside the present visible kingdom community. What he is depicting is something far more staggering and crucial for *his followers:* the terms of *this* future judgment apply unequivocally *to those who claim to know, follow, and love Emmanuel.* It means that Christ's disciples must pragmatically grasp in this world the Incarnational significance of "Emmanuel" and convert that into living practice by loving their neighbor as they love themselves — and, even more, *as they love God* (22:37-40).

Throughout the Sermon on the Mount, Jesus had made explicit the grounds for this final judgment. Good religion was elucidated: it is in essence a righteousness that exceeds that of the scribes and Pharisees, one far removed from their sort of petty, man-made, ossified, and often inhumane legal externalisms (5:19-20). The model for this true righteousness is the perfect charity of the Father (5:43-

48), made incarnate, visible, and imitable through his Son and his deeds. In the parable, the terms are stated with a clarity that should, at least from time to time, send a shock of conviction and contrition through professing believers as they read it: "Truly, I say to you, as you did it to one of the least of these my brethren, you did it to me. . . . Truly, I say to you, as you did it not to the least of these, you did it not to me" (25:40, 46). What lies behind these words is the full force of the meaning of "God with us." The realization of this truth must impel *his disciples* to become "sons of [their] heavenly Father," loving (i.e., doing good to) neighbor and enemy alike, leaving judgment in the hands of God alone, who reveals his mercy universally and indiscriminately, so that they might become "perfect [in charity], as [their] heavenly Father is perfect."

In the light of such an altered vision of humanity — a humanity joined eternally to the Lord who made it in his own image, a humanity thereby revealed to be of infinite worth, a humanity for which he died and which in his own person he raised from the bonds of death — there can be no disdain or disregard for any human being, and especially not for "the least," who are thus in need of our particular care and protection (the child, the blind, the lame, the hungry, the thirsty, the sick, the suffering, the prisoner, the stranger, and, I dare add, the unborn). In fact, in every nation to which the gospel is proclaimed, the presence of Christ is to be seen in particular in "the least of these." If there is any notion of "the body of Christ" in Matthew, or an "extension of the Incarnation," it is not so much seen *in the church* as it is seen *by the church*. No matter where they are, the followers of Christ are supposed to be those who look around them among the nations and there see Jesus — "Emmanuel" — already present and visible in the features of those to whom they minister.

For Matthew, judgment begins with the household of God. It is based not merely on a set of moral rules but on revealed "righteousness," and certain questions must inevitably arise for the professing Christian as a consequence. Who is Jesus Christ, "Emmanuel," and what does this mean for the way I live my life now? In following him, have I avoided bad religion — that is, "the leaven of the Pharisees and Sadducees"? Have I sought to live according to the ideal of perfection in love, especially as it pertains to "the least," which is the very character of the Father, as demonstrated by the Son? Do I recognize Christ in the human faces of the world in which I dwell, and do I minister to him through them? This sort of self-examination is not, certainly, to be taken as an invitation to scrupulosity or self-nagging or guilt. Such self-preoccupied feelings merely waste time and effort. Rather, this self-examination is an invitation to pragmatic faith.

Matthew does not present Christianity as just another version of religious moralism or externalism or formalism — none of which makes allowance for the real struggles, challenges, and occasional failures of Christ's disciples. Instead, it is a call to live an authentic religious existence, not one along the lines of those whom Jesus denounces so strongly in the Gospel. It is an inducement to be transformed interiorly in a way that manifests itself in genuine, practical, unsentimental love of God and neighbor.

Modern readers may dislike this tough mythological concept of "Judgment" and see in it a sort of threat to "be good — or else." Soft and fluffy versions of Christianity may dismiss it altogether as "primitive" and as a "fear tactic." On the other hand, fundamentalists of every stripe (which might include Dominicans as well as Baptists) tend to like the idea far too much (especially the "hell" part), and seem to think that believing the right doctrines rightly will be sufficient to assure eternal blessedness. Both tendencies, however, trivialize the most essential and perennial implication of the Judgment scenario.

Pragmatically speaking, our lives are either significant or they are not, and the lives of others are either significant or they are not. And, if we are trying to follow Jesus, either his humanity as "God with us" is ultimately significant or it is not. Judgment reminds us that we hold our own lives in our hands, that what we do or don't do matters, and that we Christians (of all people) should be those most willing to see human beings — all human beings — as somehow taken up and included in the human nature of Christ. It is there to sober us up. The *imagery* of the Judgment is not to be taken literally; it is parabolic, mythological, and iconic. That caveat notwithstanding, we should be very careful not to banish from our minds the whole idea of a final, definitive evaluation of our lives. Whatever the future reality of it may be, we should be prepared for it through our own ongoing reflective self-examination and consequent actions. It is a call to take our selves and other selves seriously, and to do so because we are ultimately accountable to the truest Self of all.

This is a practical doctrine. Its object is to demolish the one thing for which Jesus shows an inexorable loathing: religious hypocrisy.